But it wasn't like this in the JCR hand book

A VICTORIA

Hand Book

1982 ~ ~1983

St John's College DURHAM

Up and Down the City Walls,
In and Out the Bailey!
A light-hearted celebration of
Old Durham ...

Durham Cathedral
Saturday, November 25, 1995
7.30pm

◆ ANNIVERSARIES AND THEIR LESSONS   ◆ BIBLE TRANSLATION IN PAPUA NEW GUINEA
◆ LETTER TO THE EDITOR FROM CANON A E H RUTTER
◆ JUMBALANCE TRIP TO COLOGNE – DECEMBER 2005
◆ HENLEY ROYAL REGATTA   ◆ LETTER FROM ERIC RELS
◆ TEACHING PALESTINIAN REFUGEES IN LEBANON
◆ ST PAUL'S COLLEGE KAPSABET KENYA

ST·JOHN'S COLLEGE
DURHAM

COLLEGE
RECORD

ETS EVENTS COMMITTEE
LY PRESENTS

ailey ball

FIDES NOSTRA VICTORIA:

A Portrait of St John's College, Durham

FIDES NOSTRA VICTORIA:

A Portrait of St John's College, Durham

Edited by Amabel Craig

THIRD MILLENNIUM
PUBLISHING, LONDON

This book is dedicated to all Johnians – past, present and future.

'This is the victory that conquers the world, our faith.'

— 1 John 5:4 (NRSV)

Fides Nostra Victoria: A Portrait of St John's College, Durham

©Third Millennim Publishing

First published in 2008 by Third Millennium Publishing Limited,
a subsidiary of Third Millennium Information Limited.

2–5 Benjamin Street
London
United Kingdom
EC1M 5QL
www.tmiltd.com

ISBN: 978 1 903942 86 4

Edited by Amabel Craig
Designed by Matthew Wilson
Production by Bonnie Murray

Reprographics by Studio Fasoli, Italy
Printed by Gorenjski Tisk, Slovenia

Contents

Preface

Some of us were fortunate to be at St John's Durham for the 50th anniversary of the College and from this photograph it looks as if we celebrated by 'being counted with them that go down into the pit'. As we were always taught to preach from the text, rather than our own opinions, I thought I should get the obligatory scripture reference in right away.

Yet it is partly because of the teaching which made scripture come alive – Jim Hickinbotham on The Acts, John Cockerton giving us good reason to appreciate the Greek text – that I have remained thankful for life at Cranmer. The fact that we were made to feel part of the whole College, through sport, through worship, through social events, also made those years for me by far the happiest of my student days.

There is something about the collegiate spirit of St John's which makes it such a special place of formation for generation after generation of students. It is something that has been kept alive through many changing times. When, as Bishop of Durham, I talked and worshipped with John's men and women, I recognised that same open friendship, rigorous faith and anticipation for the adventure of life which I had caught for myself in a previous generation.

I believe that, because this book has been largely written by Johnians, it captures that spirit and is a worthy and permanent part of our centenary celebrations.

Michael Turnbull, Cranmer Hall 1958–60,
Bishop of Rochester 1988–94, Bishop of Durham 1994–2003

A Cranmer Hall visit to Amble coal mine, September 1959. Left to right: Titus Green, Lew Higdon, David Towne, Michael Turnbull, Graham Hands, Steve Tombline, Stanley Holbrooke-Jones, Dobson Heron, Chris Williams. Kneeling: Revd Peter Harrison.

In a Sentence

It feels as if they never left,
they the sum total, so far,
of a coming and going
kaleidoscopic community of formation
in walls already distinctly lived in,
particularly, historically, by more than ordinary,
characterful personalities, Durham personalities
and the pioneers of what it means to be Johnian,

never ghosts, these generations of enquiring minds,
generous hearts and free spirited fellowship,
but rather, stitches in a human tapestry,
we ourselves embedding what we already were and were to be,
a part of what is being laid down here,
for better or for worse, love it or not,
this work in progress configured by Christ and his call.

© David Grieve

Introduction

St John's College has played a significant part in my life, as it has to many others. Perhaps it's because as undergraduates, we are welcomed into a community at a time in which we need to spread our wings, to become truly independent, often in our first months away from home, but need the security of a community in which to do this.

I not only found a husband (and encouraged him to train at Cranmer), completed a degree, made some fantastic friends, but fell in love with a very special city, group of buildings and idea of a potentially disparate group of people creating a community.

It has been an honour, a pleasure and a challenge to work on this centenary book. I had to quickly learn the College's history, exactly which buildings belong to St John's, scratch the surface of the archives, talk to some amazing people, laugh at shared memories and love of the community of St John's. I have also revisited my own five years involved with St John's, and had the pleasure of staying in the heights of Cranmer for a few delightful nights.

It's strange how certain places bring memories flooding back: the smell of the library, the creaking, uneven floors, the unending corridor through College, the familiar College sweatshirts mingling in the JCR (although everyone looks so young!)

I have also been able to reflect on the victory won through faith through the century. The vision of a small group of men for a new theological training hostel in the northeast, to the first new building of Cruddas, the first bishop from John's Hall, a substantial number of missionaries, the development of

Cranmer Hall, the trailblazing admission of women, the first (and only, so far) female principal, the development of conference trade, the building of St Margaret's Garth, the Borderlands project, and so on.

The College's Principals have been men (and woman) of amazing vision and faith, steering a unique college through the trials of developing a real Christian, learning community.

As this book was written, I remembered my first year at John's, ten years previously. Each point in the year – freshers' Sunday, matriculation, the autumnal beauty of the riverbanks, formals, Bailey Ball, summer revision, and so on – seemed fresh in my memory but with the glow of a decade's experience in-between. How much more sweetly are those memories from Johnians 20, 40 or 60 years ago – and how well remembered are so many stories!

The distance of time gives a rose-tinted hue to memories. Time is most vibrantly lived in the three to four years at John's. It is an exciting and unique time in one's life.

If the College walls could talk, the stories they could tell! I have had a taste of this in my various conversations and the stories I've received, and I hope to be able to pass on a flavour of this.

Photographs included have come from archives, contributors, and commissioned photographs of College. You may notice that staff are included in quite a few photographs. Staff keep the College running, they stay longer and, it could be said, that they retain the College's collective memory. Of course, there are so many student photographs of our own friends and particularly significant moments of our 'Johnian experience'. I have tried to include a few significant photographs, but, of course, so many collections of students' photographs are untapped.

I hope you enjoy this celebratory book. Perhaps you'll see some familiar faces, learn something new about 'our' College, and relive your time at John's.

Our victory is through faith – amen!

Amabel Craig, Editor
Gateshead, November 2008

BA Theology 1997–2000; Cranmer spouse 1999–2002;
member of staff 2000–1; tutor 2003–4

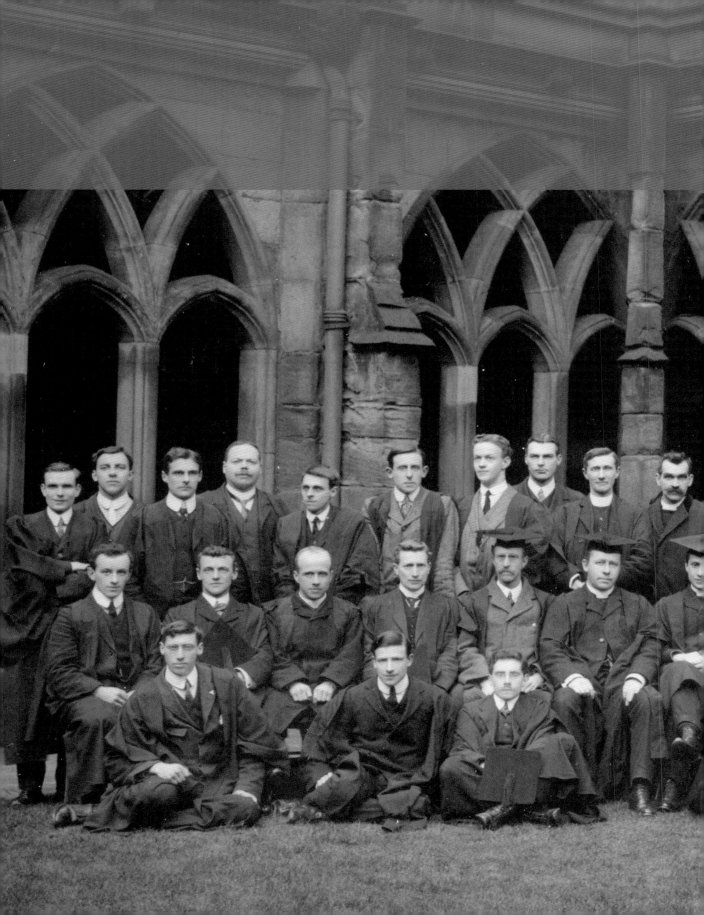

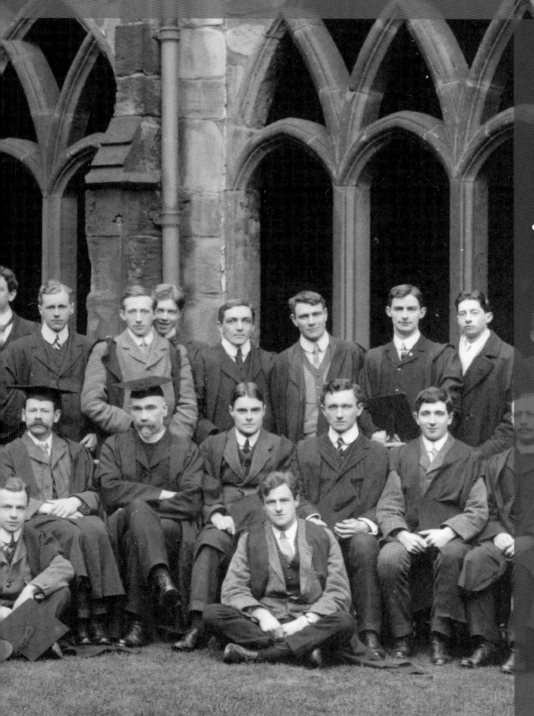

PART I

A History

Foundations Laid 1909

The vision, drive and determination of some individuals are central to the foundation of any institution to drive it forward. And so, rather than providing a detailed history of the college, which would be repeating the work of Canon Timothy Yates in *A College Remembered* (1978, 2nd edn 2000) and for which there is insufficient space here, this will be a general account of the foundation and establishment of St John's and a reflection on the unique nature of college life.

The virtual founder of 'our' St John's was Revd John Edwin Watts-Ditchfield (1861–1923), whose early biography may be found in E.N. Gowing's *John Edwin Watts-Ditchfield* (1908). It was Watts-Ditchfield's passion for evangelism, university-level training for missioners both in this country and throughout the globe and a concern to found a college in the north of England that led to a new theological college in Durham University. Yates describes him as 'first and foremost an evangelist', originally trained by the Methodist Church (the first connection between Anglicans and Methodists in St John's College), but, when he was unable to secure himself ministry overseas, he was welcomed into the Anglican

Members of First College Council

- President H. Wace, Dean of Canterbury
- Chairman Revd J.E. Watts-Ditchfield, Lord Bishop of Chelmsford
- From St John's, Highbury: Revd Dr Greenup (principal), W. Joynson Hicks,
- From St Aidan's, Birkenhead: J.P. Hargreaves, Revd F.S. Guy Warman, Revd C. Lisle Carr
- From Durham University: Revd Dr D. Dawson-Walker, Revd J. How; P.J. Heawood, G.A. Solly
- From Church Missionary Society: Revd Cyril Bardsley, Revd J.A. Lightfoot
- Others: W.D. Cruddas, Robert Armitage, Revd J.T. Inskip (vicar of Jesmond), Revd Theodore Woods (vicar of Bishop Auckland)

Church, serving in Islington and then Bethnal Green, where he 'became a leading figure in the evangelical world of his day' (Yates).

St John's ideological foundations were being laid: connections with the Church Missionary Society and Church Pastoral Aid Society, London-based evangelical institutions, combined with work among the underprivileged alongside academic achievement.

In 1907 the Archbishop of Canterbury, Randall Davidson, set up a commission, 'The Supply and Training of Candidates for Holy Orders', whose findings included a recommendation to set up church 'hostels' in university settings to provide professional training as well as a university course before ordination for non-graduate students. The seeds of the foundation of St John's Hall, Durham, were laid one evening in 1907 when Watts-Ditchfield discussed his idea of setting up a new hostel with his friends Guy Warman (a future president of the college council, Bishop of Manchester and chief inspector of the first two inspections of St John's College) and William Donaldson Cruddas. 'They went away the next morning very different men, because they saw

Opposite: A reflection of one student's life from 1919 onwards: a selection of Henry Ganderton's Johnian ephemera from the College's archives, including term cards, lecture note book, University Roll of Service, final examination question papers and ordination licences.

Above: The College crest.

Left: The de facto founder of St John's Hall, Durham, Revd J.E. Watts-Ditchfield, Bishop of Chelmsford.

Highbury St John's

Founded in 1863, St John's College, Highbury was an independent evangelical theological college in Islington, London, established for missionary training, which in turn had a close relationship with Islington College. St John's Durham has its genesis in the work of her southern namesake. Connections between the two St Johns at either ends of the country remained strong. In the 1913 issue of *The (Highbury) Johnian*, mention is made of 'Misters Chau, Bazalgette and Burdett' who will 'go up to Durham where we wish them every success'. Connections between the two colleges were further cemented when Charles Wallis, formerly tutor and Dean of St John's Highbury, joined the Durham staff in 1912 as vice-principal, chaplain, then Principal from 1919.

Watts-Ditchfield's vision on the way to fruition' (*Old Johnian*, 1930). Instead of being an offshoot of Highbury, furthering their training after two years in London, St John's Hall was established as a new, limited liability company, an independent university hall, with a capital of only £2. Also involved were Prebendary H.E. Fox with his strong Durham connections (his family home was Number 4 South Bailey, also known as Bowes House), Professor

The opening ceremony for Cruddas House in March 1913, including Miss Eleanor Cruddas ceremonially 'opening' the House in her father's name.

Dawson Dawson-Walker and Revd Charles Wallis, both future chaplains and principals of St John's Hall, who worked together to secure housing and recognition from the University of Durham.

Watts-Ditchfield was central in deciding on Durham as the location for this new hall, not least because an evangelical training college in Durham would be distinct from St Chad's Hall, established in 1904 in the Anglo-Catholic tradition. In a speech at the opening of Cruddas House in April 1913 he expressed his concern that '[St John's] Hall is for the training of men who would present the old gospel'. He also conceived and launched the college's first development fund, the 'Million Shilling Fund', shared between the 'sister' evangelical theological colleges St John's College, Highbury, St John's Hall, Durham and St Aidan's College, Birkenhead, to build and found the colleges. This elicited an anonymous gift from William Cruddas, which enabled a lease to be taken out on Number 6 South Bailey in 1909. In the following year Number 4 South Bailey was purchased; and Number 3 South Bailey (Haughton House) was purchased in 1912.

Watts-Ditchfield continued to serve as president of the college council until his death in 1923, having also served nine years as Bishop of Chelmsford. Although his name may not be as familiar as others mentioned in this history – for example, no room in the college has been named after him – all Johnians should be indebted to this man's vision and dedication to the creation and establishment of a new, unique training college in Durham.

An article in the *Old Johnian*, 1956, reflects St John's early history: 'The college's connection with St John's College, Highbury, is indicated by the inclusion of a gold lion rampant (double-tailed and crowned) on a blue field in the third quarter of the shield. The lion can be traced even further than to Highbury. The achievement of St John's Highbury is: a lion rampant ermine, crowned and armed gules [with red tongue and claws], double-tailed on a field azure. [Derived in part from the Peache family, whose lion wears a gold crown. One of the benefactors of St John's, Highbury, was a member of the Peache family, whose coat of arms is similar.] In the Michaelmas term of 1913 the coat of arms of St John's, Durham, was: quarterly, I and IV – a red cross, now known as St Cuthbert's cross, on a silver field; II and III – a gold ramping lion, wearing a gold crown, double-tailed on a blue field. The cross, which is the main feature of the university arms, signified the presence of the college in the university city, and later denoted its position as a constituent college of the university.

Each of the evangelists has been given an emblem: St John [has] an eagle. Appropriately then, in 1914, the symbol of St John, gold on a blue field, was included in the college shield, so making up its present composition, and was substituted for the lion which was originally in the second quarter.'

From a 1930 information leaflet…

'St John's College is a residential college of Durham University founded primarily for the education and training of candidates for Holy Orders, in accordance with principles of the Evangelical School of Theology in the Church of England. Students other than ordination candidates are admitted at the discretion of the principal. The college combines all the advantages of residence in a university with the corporate life and opportunity for regular devotion and studies that are to be found in a college where candidates are prepared for the sacred ministry of the Church.'

St. John's College, Durham.

THINGS REQUIRED BY A STUDENT.

1. Each Student must provide his own bed linen (i.e., 2 pairs of single-sized sheets and 2 pillow cases) and towels.

   All should be marked plainly with his name.

2. A dark coat. (See VII. "Rules for the guidance of Students.").

3. A gown. Black stuff gowns of the correct University shape may be obtained from :—

   Wm. Gray & Son, Saddler Street, Durham.
   Ede & Ravenscroft, 93 & 94, Chancery Lane, London.
   Wippell & Son, Duncannon Street, Charing Cross, London.

4. A small outfit for tea, e.g., a kettle, some cups and saucers, etc.

5. Ordinary necessary furniture is provided for each Student's room, but it is customary for a Student to have his own pictures, cushions, etc.

XI. MUSIC.

Music is allowed from 1 p.m.—5 p.m., and from 7-30—8 p.m. On Sundays it is allowed after breakfast—5 p.m. (excluding the time of Morning Prayer in the Cathedral) and from 7-45 p.m.—8-30 p.m.

Students may not have gramophones or ukeleles in the College.

XII. LIGHT, Etc.

Electric light will be available as necessary from 7 a.m. till 11 p.m. The Student must provide any further light he desires. Oil lamps must be of safety pattern.

Fuel is provided.

Each Student is given a washing book and must carefully follow out the directions enumerated in it.

Beer, wines and spirits are not allowed in the College except in the case of sickness, and only with the Principal's written permission.

Students must not enter any licensed house in Durham or the neighbourhood. This rule includes the Refreshment Rooms at Durham Station.

XIII. MEMBERSHIP OF CLUBS, Etc.

No Student in statu pupillari may join any political club or take any active part in politics.

XIV. COLLEGE TESTIMONIAL.

A Testimonial will be given at the completion of the course, and at the discretion of the Principal. The Student must at the same time repeat his affirmation that he is free from debt.

No Student, who has not obtained this certificate, is allowed to include the name of the College in a description of his training.

C. S. WALLIS,
PRINCIPAL.

AUGUST, 1930.
(THIS CANCELS ALL PREVIOUS LISTS).

St. John's College, Durham.

RULES FOR THE GUIDANCE OF STUDENTS.

Students are reminded that St. John's is both a College of the University and a place of preparation for the sacred Ministry of the Church. As such, it is of the first importance to maintain not only a healthy and vigorous College life, but also to keep its spiritual tone on the highest level. To this end, the following Rules have been drawn up; and it is expected that the student remembering the shortness of the course, and valuing this opportunity of acquiring habits of regular devotion and systematic study, will loyally and prayerfully make it his aim to keep them from the first.

I. COMMON PRAYER.

SERVICES IN THE COLLEGE CHAPEL.

WEEKDAYS.
Morning Prayer
Evening Prayer .... 7-45 a.m.
                                                          6-30 p.m.
SUNDAYS.
Holy Communion .... 8 a.m.
*Morning Prayer and Sermon (in the Cathedral)
*Evening Prayer and Sermon (in the Church ...... 11 a.m.
of St. Mary-le-Bow).................................... 6-30 p.m.
HOLYDAYS.
Holy Communion .... 7-30 a.m.

* Gowns are worn.

Left: The first property leased, later bought, by the new Hall was number 6 South Bailey in 1909.

Foundations Cemented:
Nowell Rostron and Dawson-Walker 1909–19

The University of Durham was founded in 1832. By 1909 six colleges or halls were members: University, Hatfield, St Cuthbert's Society, Bede, Hild and St Chad's. Reflecting its size as a city, Durham was not a large university – in 1908, there were only 250 members – but it expanded rapidly, growing to about 500 students in 1934. St John's Hall opened with five students, but grew rapidly, housing 11 in 1910, 40 by 1912 and 92 in 1934.

Sidney Nowell Rostron, St John's Hall's first principal, a graduate of St John's College, Cambridge, got the new hall onto its feet. In his memoirs Stanley Hinchcliffe remembers: 'I shall always be glad that I was at John's, Durham … Nowell Rostron was that rare breed, an intellectual with a genuine love of souls.

Principal Nowell Rostron.

He married [Ella] early on in his tenure of office and [she] became a leading light in the Mothers' Union.'

Nowell Rostron describes the early days in his message given to the college's 'coming of age' celebrations in 1930 (reprinted in *Old Johnian*, 1930): 'I arrived in Durham as the first principal of the new St John's Hall on Wednesday, 6 October 1909. The first students – four matriculated and one on probation – came the next day. Term began on 8 October, and the opening ceremony with the dedication of the Hall took place on the following Tuesday, 12 October. There were many problems we had to face – the fashioning of a corporate life on right lines, the creation of worthy traditions and a helpful tone and atmosphere, the establishment of our place in the general life of the university, and many others. I well recall the search for a college motto and the choice of *Fides Nostra Victoria*; the discussion with the learned antiquary and kind-hearted friend, Dr Fowler, about the college Arms and the choice (in which all members of the Hall concurred) of the college blazer.

'That first term! I can never forget it! … It is wonderful what can be done with small numbers. At the beginning of the second year we had to take in another house, unfortunately some distance away [Number 4 South Bailey], and presently we had many members living out in lodgings. It was no easy matter to foster the corporate life under these conditions, but on the whole it grew in strength and also in the spirit of brotherhood. Successes began to come in the Schools … Who that was then at the Hall will not forget all my colleagues meant to its life and work! Who can fail

First Staff

- **Principal Sidney Nowell Rostron, MA (1909–12)**
- Chaplain: Professor Dr Dawson Dawson-Walker
- Tutor (Classics): John Hartley Wadsworth
- Butler: Mr Johnson
- Cook/Housekeeper: Mrs Johnson, 'that faithful and masterful personality' (Nowell Rostron)
- Boot Boy: George

Principal Dawson Dawson-Walker.

bathing our souls … St John's has done great things. By the Divine blessing it will do still greater. There has never been more urgent need of its work than there is today.'

Although Nowell Rostron was principal for only two years, they were 'thrilling years of the first venture'. He resigned in 1911 to take up the post of vicar in Kirkdale, Liverpool. He retained his connection with St John's, commenting in his address to the 'coming of age' celebrations in 1930 that he kept his college group portraits on his study wall. On his death in 1948, he left a legacy to be shared between St John's Durham and Cambridge, and Ridley Hall.

His successor, Dawson Dawson-Walker (chaplain from 1910), summarized these years of rapid growth in a speech at the opening of Cruddas House in March 1912: 'The Hall began with a little band of five students in October 1909. Last term [Michaelmas 1912] we had 42. [By 1913 52 men could be accommodated.] The Hall, it should be remembered, is, in a very real sense, a unique institution [unlike non-graduate colleges, such as St John's, Highbury, nor a postgraduate college, like Wycliffe Hall]. St John's, Durham, represents the first occasion when the evangelical school of thought in the Church of England has founded and inaugurated a hall, which is a residential hall in one of our English universities. St John's, Durham, is one of the first signs of a readiness of the evangelical section of the Church to set its hand to the problem of providing university graduates for the ministry of the Church of England. It does not

to remember … Johnson the butler, or George the boot boy, dismissed finally each term only to turn up ready to work for nothing if he could but be kept on at the beginning of the next term? Yet there was one side of our common life that stands out supremely. I know it meant everything to me – the wonderful quiet services in the tiny old church which we were allowed to use as our Chapel … the peace of that ancient House of God

Mr Robinson, Professor of Greek.

'It is impossible to exaggerate the debt St John's Hall owes to their devoted self-sacrificing labours. They surmounted [difficulties] all most happily, and laid the foundations of what promises to be a highly successful work. With such a staff St John's Hall now goes on its way in full assurance that it will accomplish great things.'
The Record, April 1913

W.D. Cruddas

William Donaldson Cruddas was the college's most significant benefactor. In his address at the opening of Cruddas House in 1913, the Dean of Canterbury noted: 'He felt that it was of vital importance to England and to the Church of England that the principles for which that hall stood should be represented in the Church.' He donated £5,000 (worth around £215,300 today) to buy the first college properties and a further £5000 for the building of Cruddas House, the purpose-built accommodation block for 25 students, which was opened in March 1913. 'Through the munificence of Mr Cruddas, the hall is in possession of spacious and comfortable accommodation standing in its own freehold property' (Dawson-Walker at opening of Cruddas House, 1913). Watts-Ditchfield also noticed that 'when the hall was first opened it excited his liveliest interest. [Cruddas] House will bear the name of Mr Cruddas for all time – a name honoured and respected in this district as the name of a man good and true in his day and generation.'

stand in competition with all other evangelical institutions but in cooperation with them … St John's exists to provide a well-trained ministry for the Church of England.'

The Council's first choice for Nowell Rostron's replacement was Revd Dr Dawson Dawson-Walker (1912–19). He was a man of 'sound learning, [and] his teaching gifts, his careful administration have counted for much, but to those who knew him best there counted more his simple piety, his sterling loyalty, his unselfish helpfulness and his never-failing good-tempered friendship … He was a good man and his work and his friendship made men feel glad' (Guy Warman). Dawson-Walker 'carried [St John's] through from a rather precarious infancy to the beginnings of robust adult life' (Guy Warman). He was a 'scholar with an international reputation and was a kind and helpful man' (Stanley Hinchcliffe). Alongside him as vice-principal from October 1912 was Charles Wallis: 'one hears on all hands in Durham of the strong spiritual influence he is exercising upon the students' (*The Record*, April 1913).

The First World War signalled a time of change for St John's Hall. Inevitably, the loss of six members killed in action was felt personally by everyone, as were the decrease in the number of students and domestic staff, rationing and post-war shortages. It would be difficult for anyone to serve as head of a university college when all able men were conscripted, but it must had been doubly difficult for the principal of a theological training college to be expected to provide support and reassurance to local

congregations in addition to preparing candidates for ordination and their wider missionary work.

Perhaps the burden of steering college through wartime was too heavy. 'The end of the war found him a tired man and in a state of perplexity over the running of the college' (Wallis, *Old Johnian*, 1934). Dawson-Walker resigned as principal after being offered the appointments as Canon Residentiary of Durham Cathedral and University Professor of Divinity. He remained on the college council until 1922. The reaction to his departure reflects his popularity: 'There was great pride that the honour – so well deserved – had fallen to him, but even the comforting thought of the glory reflected on the college, failed to obliterate the deep regret which was felt at losing the wise guidance and genial presence of the 'Head' (*Old Johnian*, 1912). '[Dawson-Walker] remained always a staunch friend who rang true, a man who was exceedingly unselfish and who possessed genuine piety which was no less real because it was tempered with humour and a strong love of the human side of things' (Wallis, *Old Johnian*, 1934).

It seems fitting that one of Dawson-Walker's final acts was the granting of college status to St John's Hall after only ten years. The college council commented: 'Under his principalship the college speedily attained a foremost position in the university. Unfortunately, the prospects full of promise were dimmed and marred by the years of war; yet in spite of the tremendous difficulties which this entailed, the college … under his wise leadership is already recovering from the strain and effects of war.'

The Wallis Years 1919–45

'To one and all we tender our hearty thanks for the help given.'

– Charles Wallis, *Old Johnian*, 1926

The end of the war and the departure of Dawson-Walker marked the start of a new phase of college life. After three principals in ten years, St John's now had a long-serving hand at the helm to steer the college through the storms facing post-war Britain. St John's was increasing in size – in student numbers, buildings and reputation – and this was to a large extent due to the reputation of Principal Wallis.

Charles Wallis had an impressive curriculum vitae. He had experience of war service as a chaplain on a hospital ship and a high reputation as Dean of St John's, Highbury, then as Dean of Music at

Principal's Fact File

- **Principal Charles Steel Wallis**
- Former positions Chaplain, vice-principal (1912–19)
- Academic expertise Music
- Vice-principals H. Hughes (1919–21), H.Y. Ganderton (1924–9), J.C. Hawthorn (1931–3), O.A.C. Irwin (1934–43)
- Chaplains H.Y. Ganderton (1920–9), E.W.P. Ainsworth (1929–32), C.H.G. Davey (1933–6), V.G. Davies (assistant, 1936–8), C. Smith (1939–45)
- Bursars H.Y. Ganderton (1921–9), W.H.A. Learoyd (1929–39), C. Smith (1939–45)
- Vice-Chancellors John Pemberton (1918–20), Sir David Drummond (1920–2), Professor Arthur Robinson (1922–4), Sir Theodore Morison (1924–6), Professor Percy Heawood (1926–8), Sir Thomas Oliver (1928–30), Revd Professor Henry Ellershaw (1930–2), Sir William Sinclair Marris (1932–4), Revd Stephen Moulsdale (1934–6), Sir Robert Bolam (1934–7), Professor Sir James Fitzjames Duff (1937–60) alternating with Rt Hon. Lord Eustace Percy (until 1952)
- Bishops of Durham Herbert Hensley Henson (1920–39), Alwyn Terre Petre Williams (1939–52)

Durham. He was a greatly respected and well-liked member of staff at Highbury between 1903 and 1912. According to the appreciation speech reported in *The (Highbury) Johnian* in 1920, he had a large circle of friends who appreciated his 'caustic wit'. When he left 'no adequate representation of our personal regard and appreciation towards him could be expressed tangible or otherwise'. He was going to 'pioneer work; there were no traditions and no past at St John's Hall, Durham: it had only just started: things were being moulded, he was helping to lay a new railway track'.

Charles Wallis was unafraid of a full timetable, shown by the number of appointments and positions he held during his time in Durham: no less than 16 separate positions between 1920 and 1945, including membership of University Senate, Durham Colleges Council, Faculties of Theology and Arts, Dean of Music and Principal of Durham Colleges Council. He also maintained his London connections, serving as associate of Music at Trinity College, London. He also held the position of Examining Chaplain to the Lord Bishops of Durham and Lord Bishop of Sodor and Man.

College Butler, Henry Dennison (second left).

'St John's, I found, was a small college. Indeed the whole Durham end of the university was numerically at a low ebb so soon after the end of the war. There were about 32 students of one kind and another. All the other colleges by present standards were small'
H.S. Wilkinson (1920–5), *Fides*, 1981

Wallis was an obvious choice for principal of 'St John's Number 2', having served as vice-principal and chaplain from 1912. He had deputized as principal for a term in 1919, but was appointed principal for the Church Missionary Society (CMS) missionary training college by the term's end. It took the might of three diocesan bishops, all closely involved with St John's (Moule of Durham, Watts-Ditchfield of Chelmsford and Warman of Truro), to release him from his commitment, but he continued to be involved with global mission from his Durham base. 'His zeal for the missionary cause was an inspiration to many to serve the Church overseas … he kept up a large correspondence with those who were serving abroad in all parts of the world' (Ganderton in Wallis's 1959 obituary).

Later generations of Johnians have the impression of Wallis as a strict patrician, turning off the College's electricity supply at 11pm each night, although this was a practice common to all institutions. Indeed, the picture hanging in Haughton, which has shaped most people's impression of him, 'gives the impression of the pursed lips and pince-nez of a Victorian spinster' (Yates, *A College Remembered*, p.23). It reappeared on college photos in the 1980s, at the suggestion of tutor Michael Vasey. (It is difficult to imagine what Wallis would have made of the long hair of undergraduates of both sexes.) However, H.S. Wilkinson (undergraduate in 1920–5) remembers Wallis thus: 'I cannot

speak too highly of "Charlie" Wallis. He had a very good mind and was an excellent teacher, and did much to strengthen the college. He was a most spiritually minded man, utterly devoted to St John's. But he was also an excellent organizer and rumour has it that was why he was appointed. The college was in low water financially after the war, and he did much to remedy this, especially through securing the continued interest of the Cruddas family in the college. He was an Evangelical but a man of broad Christian sympathies, and a great supporter of CMS.'

Wallis was an inclusive evangelical Anglican with a great passion for gospel proclamation both home and abroad. He was heavily involved with local open-air missions and summer camps. His social concern and passion for education were underpinned

by prayer. He pragmatically urged his students to join with him in 'remembering each other before the Throne of Grace' as they faced the reality that 'life is full of problems' (*Old Johnian*, 1926). His pragmatic spiritual advice is memorably summarized in an urge to students to remain committed to moral and church principles that could be applied to most situations: 'A wobbler is of no use to anybody' (*Old Johnian*, 1936).

Wallis's most pressing duty when he took up his post was to renovate college buildings, as described in his first principal's letter of 1919: 'Practically all my energy has been spent this last half year on the work of "reconstruction". The college was in a shocking state of dilapidation … Cruddas House has been reopened, decorated from top to bottom, and with the rest of the college, is resplendent in a coat of new paint. (The passers-by in the Bailey have stood and gaped with amazement!)' However, many buildings were shut down as numbers fell in the mid-1940s. Significant building developments included the oak panelling in Haughton dining room in 1928 (a generous gift from Henry Ganderton), expanded by the addition of a bay window in 1930. The library was increased from the original 500 books in 1909, to around 3,000 'standard works' in the 1920s.

By now students were admitted to study education and science; accommodation could be offered on the Bailey for 50 students, in addition to the principal and two resident staff. St John's had a good reputation both academically and pastorally. Canon S. Lawrence Brown (then Dean of Westminster) was so

Above: Six members of St John's died in the First World War. A total of 13 Johnians served in the armed forces, 10 as missionaries.

Left: Members of St John's College at the University's centenary reunion 1932 –
Back Row: C.K. Pattinson, S. Walker, G. Greenfield, F. Britton, H. Hinkley, J.M.R. Wright, R.S. Chapman, R. Cartwright, V.G. Davies, F.C. Waghornf, S. Bell.
Middle Row: E. Dawson-Walker, N. Maddison, G.T. Chappell, R.M. Parsons, E. Bush, Rev. A.R. Winnet, Rev. O.A.C. Irwin, H. Tuff, G.K. Muir, W.H. Learoyd, E.B. Glass, A.T. Wright.
Seated: E.F. Hudson, R. Stephens, L. King, H.S. Wilkinson, Bishop Johnson, The Principal, Rev. P.R. Frost, W.J.H. Davidson, E.P. Ainsworth, E. Sharpe, A. Goss.

Right: 'Mr O[swald] Whaley proves his versatility to every new generation of Johnians ... he never seems to be at a loss when faced with some awkward question – he is equal to all demands. "Like the brook he goes on for ever." Long may it be possible to say this, for the College reaps much benefit from his exceptional powers of tuition ...'

(Durham Johnian, 1930)

impressed during a visit that in 1927 he wrote a letter to all Johnians describing 'the spirit of cheery fellowship which pervades the college ... You seem to have at Durham an admirable combination of the intellectual, social, athletic and devotional aspects of college life ... I would urge upon all who have received a training such as is given at St John's the duty of doing their best to extend to others the privilege which they themselves have enjoyed.'

The bishop's inspectors, chaired by Bishop Guy Warman, gave St John's a positive report on their first visit in 1921, commenting on the 'friendly and harmonious [relationship between staff and students] ... all that can be desired'. St John's was recommended to be officially recognized as a training college for ordinands. A total of 58 men were in residence and prepared 'adequately' for ordination with a two-year Diploma of Theology. College finances were secured by Dora Cruddas's endowment of £9,000.

A pattern of services, both daily and weekly, had been established in St Mary-the-Less and comment was made that although attendance was required at only 50 per cent of the services, 'many men hardly miss a service'. Overall, the inspectors found 'a very favourable impression of the tone and conduct of the college' – high praise for a fledgling college.

Oswald W. Whaley, known as Old Whaley, joined as Classical Lecturer in 1921 'and ever since that time his genial personality and unique laugh have endeared themselves to several generations of students ... It has been said of Mr Whaley that he will successfully coach a man in any subject, provided that he is given a book on the subject and 48 hours' notice ... How many times have we heard the well-known phrase, "If it hadn't been for old Whaley, I should never have got through"' (an appreciation in *Old Johnian*, 1929, by E. W. P. Ainsworth, assistant chaplain).

Principal Wallis's longevity and devotion to St John's is reflected in the number of senior staff he 'outlived': four vice-principals, five chaplains and three bursars.

An Appreciation of Canon Wallis

'Canon Wallis was a man of unflagging energy, whose orderly and disciplined life enabled him to get through a vast amount of work, and yet leave time for social engagements, and for personal contacts with his own men in college. He had a keen and critical eye ... but he was also quick to encourage. He set himself a very high standard in all that he did, and expected others to aim high also. He had great gifts and outstanding qualities of character; a man of great intellectual and spiritual strength, but nevertheless of real humility, possessing an inner harmony which saved him from the arrogance that exaggerates personal capacity, and from the ambition which overleaps itself ... His influence impressed itself very deeply upon the life of the college, and very many who were there under Canon Wallis owe to his sincerity of purpose – so evident in his teaching and example – a deepening of their own spiritual life, and a more purposeful outlook. His was a dedicated life, and as someone once said to me: "It did you good to be with him." He was always dependable and approachable ... He was full of kindness, and those of us who were privileged to know him well will never forget his friendliness, his humour and his zest for life'

H. Y. Ganderton, Obituary in *Durham Johnian*, 1959

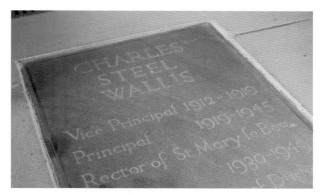

Principal Wallis' ashes were interred under the chancel step in the College chapel where a memorial stone was laid.

The arrival of another war in 1939 had an impact on college, but not as severe or damaging an impact as the First World War. On the whole, numbers in the university fell no lower than 75 per cent of the total student body in 1939 – that is, 400 students. By 1945 Johnian numbers reduced from 90 to a low of 12, but college was far from empty. During the 1940s RAF cadets were based in Durham while they were undertaking physics and maths training, and Cruddas House was used as overspill accommodation when University College and Hatfield College were full. The testosterone-fuelled young men were replaced by female undergraduates from the newly expanding St Mary's College. (Female undergraduates were usually accommodated at Neville's Cross College, St Hild's and St Mary's, and numbers increased as they were allowed to continue their education during the war.) St Mary's buildings were also used by the RAF – they had excellent views over the strategic Prebends Bridge – so while their new buildings were erected over the river, some students were housed in Cruddas until 1945.

Wallis was made a Canon in 1937, which he described as 'a pop gun [to] fire occasionally on behalf of St John's'. On his departure from St John's in 1938 he wrote to all Old Johnians (by now there were more than 300) that he was 'overwhelmed with kindness' at his leaving gifts, a set of volumes on music and 50 guineas: 'I fear there was much exaggeration of the value of my work during the past 26 years, but I was greatly encouraged by the warmth of affection and goodwill of Old Johnians … I felt I was the "Father" of a very large and affectionate family. The experience was humbling too, for it recalled the many instances when I had made mistakes and failed. Please forgive me those. It is never too late to mend and I must set to work in this direction during the time that is left to me' (*Old Johnian*, 1938). Wallis continued to be involved in college life, personally editing the college newsletter and maintaining regular correspondence with alumni. He served as rector of St Mary-le-Bow until 1949.

He died on 6 June, 1959, only days before St John's jubilee celebrations on 23 June. The funeral service was held in St Mary-le-Bow Church, and it was conducted by Canon Henry Ganderton, the rector, the Revd Owen T. Owen, Canon H.E.W. Turner and Principal Hickinbotham. A memorial service was held in college on 18 June. Hickinbotham remembers in the *Durham Johnian* of 1960: '[Wallis's] interest in St John's was eager right to the end. The college was his life's work, and I suppose that it owes more to him than to any other individual.' Further warm tribute was paid by Michael Ramsey, then Archbishop of York, in his sermon at the college's jubilee: 'Charlie Wallis made the place of St John's secure, led it to prestige and influence within the university and gave to so many the impress of his kindly wisdom, his generosity of spirit, his strength of conviction, his wit and his love for music.'

Wallis's service to St John's had spanned an important time in the history of both the college and the nation. He steered the college through the aftermath of the First World War, rebuilding confidence and establishing a strong reputation ecclesiastically, academically and athletically.

In October 1919, Mr J.H. Wadsworth, the College's Classical Tutor since 1909 and Censor from 1912, died. He was also University Lecturer in Education. He was an enthusiastic cricketer, keen lawn tennis player and a boat club coach. A memorial tablet was erected to his memory in the chapel from donations from Johnians.

Student Numbers	
1909	5
1918	7
1919	45
1921	58
1927	62
1929	70
1934	78
1945	12

War and Welfare:
Williams's Reconstruction 1945–54

After the strong hand of St John's 'man of steel', Charles Wallis, the new principal was ready to build on the strong foundations greatly shaken during the Second World War.

Ronald R. Williams shared with his predecessors a distinguished academic reputation, this time begun at Cambridge, where, like Nowell Rostron before him, he won the Carus New Testament Greek Theology Prize. He trained at Ridley Hall, Cambridge, served his curacy in Leyton and returned to Ridley Hall as chaplain (1931–4). He was 'home secretary' for CMS, with particular responsibility for education (1934–40), after which he worked in the religious division of the Ministry of Information. Williams was installed as the fourth principal of St John's College on 15 October 1945 at a service at St Mary-the-Less, where the distinguished guests included H.T. Vodden, president of the college council and Bishop of Hull,

Professor A. Michael Ramsey, then head of the Theology Department, and James Duff, warden of Durham colleges.

Unlike the bachelor Charles Wallis, Williams was married to Cecily, whose lively memoirs, *A Bishop's Wife, But Still Myself* (1961), includes a description of their 'happy, liberty-loving life' of nine years at St John's. She remembers that 'the welcome we received at St John's would have melted a heart of stone. Matron had prepared a room for us in her house and there were hot baths and a delicious dinner awaiting us … I liked Mrs Dennison [the butler's wife]; we became friends at once and I was always popping over to see Mrs Dennison in their pretty little house next to the college chapel [the parsonage].'

It is perhaps significant that this principal was married because an increasing number of married students joined the College following the forces' return from the war. Cecily remembers: 'Our first batch of students were ex-servicemen almost to a man, and many of them were of our age group.' She started a fellowship for wives (and fiancées) as they prepared to adjust to their future ministry together.

Ronald and Cecily Williams walking in the college grounds with their spaniel Westcott.

Many students came to Durham to continue training for ordination after having been in the forces, often after two years' National Service, sometimes several years after taking their first degrees.

Neil Robinson remembers: 'I arrived at Durham in October 1949 in a relaxed and happy mood, on demob leave. From the start St John's was a warm, friendly and cheerful place. There was such a wide variety of experience, interests and abilities around that I revelled in the richness of it all. I quickly sensed that we had come from different backgrounds and long, different routes but were sharing together in an understanding of the privilege of being there. Faith was much more than I had known it to be. It belonged to us all: it was exhilarating! … Inevitably there were groupings of close friendships arising from areas of accommodation, academic work, sport, the wide range of debate, music and theatre or from religious interests and enthusiasms. Such friendships underpinned the general sense of belonging.'

Williams's objective when taking up office was 'to make the college a real home of learning and not only a hostel for university students' and 'to provide a carry-on where a wide spectrum of students coming out of the forces could feel at home and at peace and in this I think we succeeded'. This 'home' and 'peace' resulted in a dramatic increase in numbers during William's principalship: from only 12 in 1945 to 103 students in 1953, with more than 90 students in college for most years.

Memories of 'R.R.'

Williams appears to have been a well-liked principal, known to his students as 'R.R.', or 'the Prin'. Neil Robinson (Senior Man 1953–4) remembers: 'R.R. Williams brought with him considerable pastoral experience and an acute theological mind. The tasks he faced were considerable too. It was his responsibility to select both staff and students for the college and to build up its numbers from the 40 students he inherited. At the same time he had to combine the responsibility of the college as both a theological college of the Church of England and a constituent college of the university.

'I certainly found him to be helpful, friendly and even fatherly. He was always good company with an enjoyable sense of humour. He had a quite subtle and gentle way of suggesting a course of action that he thought might work well and of proffering an equally gentle rebuke if he thought it necessary … One evening, three students, returning from an obviously enjoyed time in town, found the college door locked and so proclaimed the biblical message that "the gates of Hell shall not prevail against thee", only to have the principal open the door to let them in. I also recall a great friend's reading of a particularly gruesome Old

Ronald and Cecily in Durham receiving news of Ronald's appointment at Bishop of Leicester in September 1953.

Testament story after the manner of, and in the style, of "Listen with Mother" to the vast enjoyment of the students, but to the great displeasure of the principal. I think with great pleasure and amusement of Edgar Landen's playing of the chapel organ and especially of his rendition of "The Arrival of the Queen of Sheba" to accompany the exit of principal and staff from Chapel.'

Leslie Stanbridge (ordinand 1947–9; chaplain 1951–5) remembers 'R.R.' as a 'splendid colleague'. Like a 'commanding officer', he was never familiar and kept his distance, which suited that generation and 'made for a happy place'.

Attracting good-calibre students to Durham created the 'glory age' of the Theology Department. As Cecily Williams remembers: 'Ronald loved his life as principal and was delighted to be consorting once more with theologians [lecturing on NT, publishing his commentary on Acts in 1953]. The Theological Faculty was a vintage group and included three of Ronald's close friends – Michael Ramsey [head of department], Alan Richardson and Sammy Greenslade [and C.K. Barrett and H.E.W. Turner as Lightfoot Professor].' The good relationship between St John's and the Theology Department was shown in 1949 when the department granted a 9am lecture-free period three times a week specifically so that ordinands could attend lectures in-house in St John's, a feature that remained into the 1960s.

The staff often arranged a college mission at the end of the long vacation. Members of college included a number of different nationalities: Nigerians, Norwegians, Finns and Germans. In

Transforming worship

John Millyard remembers Principal Williams 'transforming' worship at St John's: 'When I joined the college in 1949 the chapel looked decidedly dreary: drab walls, and insignificant little 'holy table' with no frontal and no candles, inadequate rails and no sanctuary carpet. In 1950–1 Ronnie Williams decided to alter all this: the walls were whitened, the sanctuary carpeted, new rails and a beautiful Laudian crimson damask frontal thrown over the altar and crowned with tall candles and cross; the *Public School Hymnal* gave way to the 1950 *Hymns Ancient and Modern*, and we learned how to sing speech rhythm (quite an innovation in those days). It was a transformation – the chapel would have graced anything in Oxford or Cambridge, and it was a joy to go and worship!'

particular Heinz Kuhn came over as a German refugee and is remembered fondly. Cecily Williams recalls that he became 'a great friend' to the Williamses and that Ronald was godfather to his child.

Barzillai Beckerleg replaced Dougie Michell as chaplain. 'He was,' says John Rogan, 'a man of sardonic wit, whose conversation sharpened our own,' while Neil Robinson

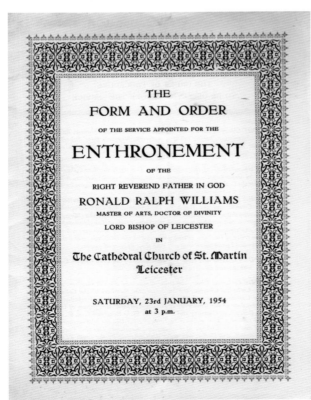

THE
FORM AND ORDER
OF THE SERVICE APPOINTED FOR THE
ENTHRONEMENT
OF THE
RIGHT REVEREND FATHER IN GOD
RONALD RALPH WILLIAMS
MASTER OF ARTS, DOCTOR OF DIVINITY
LORD BISHOP OF LEICESTER
IN
The Cathedral Church of St. Martin
Leicester

SATURDAY, 23rd JANUARY, 1954
at 3 p.m.

remembers that he 'always seemed to see the humorous side of things'. 'The chaplain [Beckerleg] kept a supply of "medicinal sherry" and was most liberal in both diagnosis of need and prescription of medicine! Barzillai was a great help to men like me who had neither expected nor been prepared for a university education,' remembers John Oliver. 'His friendship, counsel and above all his sense of humour made life that much more enjoyable.'

Williams softened the 'evangelicalism' of college, in chapel worship at least. He was a 'liberal evangelical' fully ready to keep up a distinctive evangelical note in the college', attempting the 'maintenance of [the] evangelical tradition … within a setting of representative Anglicanism' (Yates), which was illustrated by the introduction of candles into chapel worship, now eastwards facing, and the wearing of hood and scarf vesture during chapel worship.

Much work went into improving the general appearance of college buildings. The chapel was 'beautified'; Haughton dining room's bay window was extended by January 1945; Number 5 South Bailey was bought; the frontage of Numbers 2–7 South

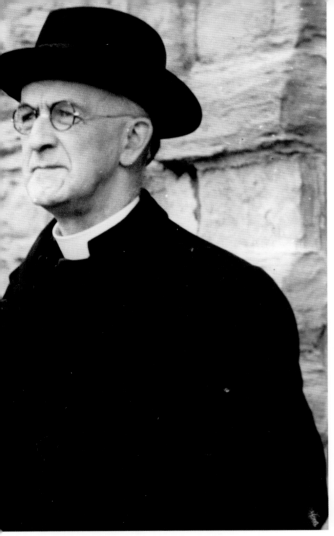

Left: Williams and Archbishop Fisher during a visit to Durham.

Bottom: College photographer, Miss Edis, setting up the 1949 photograph on what is now Cranmer lawn.

future, not unnaturally, looked bright and thrilling to him … The men were on the steps to see us off and Matron burst into tears as she kissed me goodbye … Back in Durham [after 'R.R.'s consecration] we spent a truly fantastic six weeks. Almost every day was packed with happenings; all so gay and yet all so sad because we were doing everything for the last time … The men, of course, were having the time of their lives; to have their principal already a bishop meant a lot to a college full of ordinands, and we were tremendously touched by their obvious pride in him. The college concert was the best ever and was based almost entirely on Ronald's elevation to the episcopate … There was an enormous party for Johnians past and present, at which Ronald was presented with his [pectoral] cross and ring [from funds raised by Johnians past and present]; the cross was a replica of that which he had had designed for the altar at the college chapel.'

This pectoral cross was treasured by Williams as a 'sign that I shall still carry you all in my heart [which] will remind me of that warm family life of St John's by which I have been prepared for my task', which is 'giving me away' to Leicester' (*Durham Johnian*, 1954).

Bailey was extended; and a capstone was presented to college embossed with the college's coat of arms, a generous gift from L. V. Peters, bursar and tutor.

Neil Robinson remembers: 'We shared in the jubilation and optimism of the new Queen's coronation in early June [1952] but almost as spectators as it was examination time. In college life too there were great changes at the helm. Our principal was formally offered the bishopric of Leicester in September 1953 and the announcement [was] made on 2 October, just as the new academic year was beginning. On behalf of the students I presented him with his episcopal ring, which I told him "married him to his new work". We truly wished him well.'

Cecily Williams remembers the overlap term caused by the Queen's coronation visit to Australia: 'Term began and the opening tea party with all our undergraduates we found a tremendous emotional strain. Next term there would be another tea party with the same excited buzz of conversation, the telling of stories, the leg-pulling and the outpouring of news, and everyone would be there – everyone but us. Ronald hated leaving his college, but the

Expansion and Extension:
James Hickinbotham 1954–70

St John's had an interregnum for two terms with the then vice-principal, Geoffrey Cuming, as acting principal. He was, remarks Neil Robinson (Senior Man 1953–4), 'appropriately content to keep things ticking over and on an even keel'.

Although small in stature, James Hickinbotham had a giant's vision for St John's. His successor, John Cockerton, remembers that at a much later stage he confessed that he was dedicated to the expansion of the institutions in which he served. His dynamism achieved the expansion of St John's, including the development of Cranmer Hall.

Hickinbotham read history and theology at Oxford (firsts in both) before becoming assistant curate in London and Leicester. He then became, successively, chaplain of Wycliffe Hall, acting chaplain of Wadham College, vice-principal of Wycliffe Hall (1945–50), then Professor of Theology at the University of Gold Coast (now Ghana).

Principal's Fact File

- **Principal James (Jim) Hickinbotham**
- Marital status: married to Ingeborg (Inge), née Manger; 3 children
- Vice-principals: A.G. Widdess (1955–6), Ronald Reeve (Cranmer Hall from 1958)
- Chaplain and Bursar: P.G.S. Harrison (1956–9)
- Censor: W.N. (Bill) Read
- Warden: J.C.P. Cockerton from 1968, tutor from 1958
- Tutor: A.M. Fairhurst
- Vice-Chancellors: Professor Sir James Fitzjames Duff (1937–60), alternating with Rt Hon. Lord Eustace Percy (until 1952) and Dr Charles Ion Carr Bosanquet, Professor Sir Derman Christopherson (1960–79), alternating with Dr Charles Ion Carr Bosanquet (until 1963)
- Bishops of Durham: Michael Ramsey (1952–6), Maurice Henry Harland (1956–66), Ian Thomas Ramsey (1966–72)

He was principal at a pivotal point in the college's history. It was 'a time of vigorous statesmanship with the increase of buildings, students and teaching staff, with care for scholarship, mission and devotion' (Michael Ramsey in a review of *A College Remembered* in *The Churchman*, 1982). Hickinbotham did not underestimate the challenges before him when he commented that: 'To undertake the principalship is an exhilarating and frightening experience.' He aimed for 'the maintenance of the evangelical tradition within a setting of representative Anglicanism' (quoting his predecessor, R.R. Williams).

The university was expanding rapidly, doubling in size between 1961 and 1967, and this was reflected in the extensive building throughout the city. St Mary's new buildings were finished, and new colleges

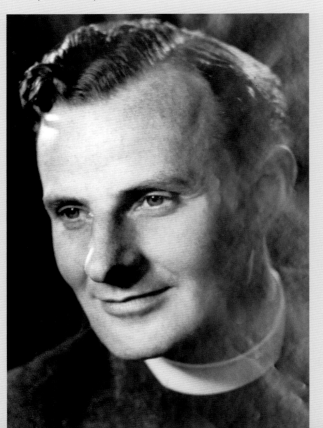

Left: Principal Hickinbotham.

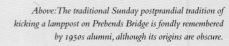

Above: The traditional Sunday postprandial tradition of kicking a lamppost on Prebends Bridge is fondly remembered by 1950s alumni, although its origins are obscure.

Growing up in St John's: A Child's Perspective

My parents came from a post in West Africa, where my father was working, straight to the northeast of England. My mother, Inge, arrived with a five-year-old son (Stephen), an 18-month-old daughter (Joy) and heavily pregnant with her third child (Philip). There was no accommodation for a principal with a family, so they lived with the matron in her quarters in South Bailey until a flat was arranged within the college – with its own front door of Number 4. From a child's perspective it was a great place to live, particularly in the vacations.

We knew the vacation was coming when the students' trunks started collecting in the lower corridor, and we immediately started playing games with them – making camps under and obstacle courses over them. Once we decided it would be funny if we changed around the labels on the trunks; as children we had no concept of the possible consequences of this game! Luckily, the rail operators noticed that the labels stuck to the trunks differed from the labels tied to them. My father was phoned. He had to stand up at the start of formal dinner and ask all the students to trek up to the station and check the labels on their trunks before they could be delivered because of his children's 'prank'. There were also great games of hide and seek in the dark around the student halls in the vacation – I can still remember the thrill and the fright of it.

The college was an intrinsic part of our life. My father left the house for chapel in the morning and had dinner in college at night … We were always answering the phone and the door to a stream of visitors, many from Africa. I remember the Nwankitis staying with us for some time and Mrs Nwankiti giving birth to a daughter in our spare room! Christmas always saw others joining us at dinner because neither parent would let someone feel lonely or out of things if they could do something about it. Because Durham is so small we had considerable freedom to go off on our bikes or on foot and meet up with friends elsewhere. This changed for a period when a new member of staff from Canada joined the staff – Ronald Reeve – who had three sons and a daughter. The boys were our ages and they lived in another part of the college. We became great friends and partners in crime! One of the boys proposed to me (I was only eight) and I cried when they left. It was a great

The Hickinbotham family outside Cruddas House: Inge carrying Philip (left) and Joy, Jim and Stephen.

childhood and a testament to my parents that although they had a high profile within Durham we never felt that we had any status to live up to. They kept an open home, which was extended to our friends as we grew up, and at the next stage of our life in Oxford several came to live with us for short periods when going through difficult times.

[Inge Hickinbotham is still alive and well, into her nineties and has very fond memories of their time at St John's.]

Joy Wishlade (née Hickinbotham)

---

were opened: Grey (1959), St Aidan's (1964), Van Mildert (1967) and Trevelyan (1968). The most populous part of the university moved off the 'peninsula', the distinctive students' union lecture rooms at Elvet Riverside and Kingsgate footbridge providing a link between the Bailey and 'hill colleges'.

St John's also grew rapidly. In 1954 there were 100 students, 83 of whom were ordinands, representing a reasonable proportion of the university's 1,200 students, although it couldn't

last. In 1963 there were 147 students; in 1969 there were 207, but a proportional diminishment to the university's total, a handicap felt particularly in sport. Despite this, Hickinbotham proudly reported in 1965 that St John's had won the cricket trophy twice in three years.

Alan Clark remembers that '1960 was the last year when there were ex-National Servicemen in the freshman group. To many of us the gap in maturity between those who had spent a

The Highs and Lows of a Chaplain's Wife

Some memories: 'Living in a flat in No. 5 through which students had access to the bathroom, etc. on the top floor. The heating going off in the middle of December, not to come on again until next term. The boiler man brought us a bucket of coal every day. Babysitters were no problem – always a ready supply of men and their girlfriends, happy for extra time together to hold hands … Being invited to join in some student events, including the Guy Fawkes night, when some of our African students objected strongly to burning an effigy. Until the arrival of a new housekeeper, the men had First World War iron bedsteads and hair mattresses and awful army grey blankets, and in some rooms coal fires, all looked after by 'bedders' (lovely ladies). Definitely no en suite! Being paid once a term – imagine one-third of the stipend lasting from June to December! We had accounts with the grocers and butchers in the city. I remember the first time ladies were allowed into hall for the Christmas dinner. We were given a packet of porage [sic] oats because the chaplain couldn't be seen until he turned east for the Creed, which also led to him being given a cardboard traffic bollard, which lit up and the message was 'Don't cross here' (we were very Protestant in those days). I remember sending on a wooden box riddled with tiny holes and smelling of stale fish to one of the African students (it was his Christmas delicacy) and taking a phone call from Durham station to say that there were freight charges of £700 to pay by our Armenian student who had been advised to send his books by air.'

Hazel Harrison   *Revd Peter Harrison, Chaplain 1956–9 and tutor.*

couple of years sitting on remote airfields or fighting terrorists in Malaya and Cyprus and those, like me, straight from school was a salutary lesson. Their more measured approach to college life, their social skills and general maturity had a significant impact on all our lives in John's. It determined me, and several others, to head for the colonies for a year or two after graduation to try to acquire that polish.'

'I came to appreciate the principal's counsel and to value him as a teacher and as the driving force behind the development of the college,' says Richard Haigh (ordinand 1954–9). 'I exchanged friendly letters with him on his retirement. However, he was a shy man, and moreover he was known by some to be troubled with the occasional return of malaria caught when he was in the tropics.'

Brian Wisken (1955–8) remembers: 'Jim Hickinbotham was a little man but with strong views about many things, including gambling. At one question and answer session one student asked Jim what he would do if someone won £75,000 on the football pools and then offered it to the college. Jim was silent for a moment, a small grin came into his face and then he said, "Try me!"'

Undoubtedly the most significant change to college occurred in 1958 with the establishment of Cranmer Hall as a distinct but integral part of the college, based in Numbers 4–7 South Bailey, with a separate library, dining room and common room. (John's Hall was principally occupying Haughton House and Cruddas House.) It was hoped that undergraduates who graduated from

John's Hall would form the 'backbone' of Cranmer Hall, although it was open to other graduates and non-graduates.

Hickinbotham worked towards maintaining the distinction between two aspects of college life: 'The undergraduate St John's likewise has its own ground and buildings, its own staff and its own way of life. It occupies Haughton and Cruddas Buildings, with the Cottage, and owns the quadrangle on which they open. Besides the traditional dining hall and JCR, an undergraduate library, a reading room, and a lecture room, and a new SCR have been established in the large rooms at the south side of Haughton' (Principal's Letter, 1958).

Hickinbotham's gift for understatement can be appreciated from his comment that 'apart from Asian 'flu we have had a normal and useful year' (Principal's Letter, January 1958). Residential nursing staff were called in and many students were seriously affected during the 1958–9 outbreak, but, evidently, the college recovered and continued to be 'useful'. Tom Thompson remembers: 'John's suffered as did many places. Many of us were patients for up to a couple of weeks in the JCR in Haughton. Quite an experience – especially as we were all afraid of the college doctor, Dr Macdonald, who had a reputation for being very fond of whisky and whose diagnoses were never really trusted as a result.'

Paul Conder, a tutor in the 1960s, remembers: 'Jim Hickinbotham was a person of great vision and enterprise.

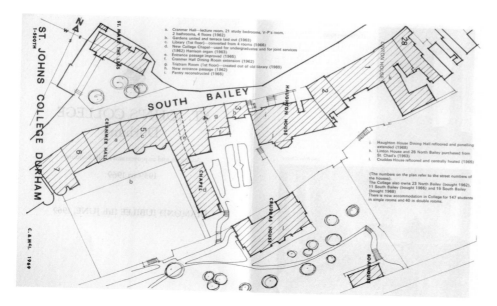

A major development appeal was launched in St John's Jubilee year, 1959 to provide new accommodation and an undergraduate chapel (ordinands continued to use St Mary-the-Less). The appeal lasted until College's Diamond Jubilee year but its effects were already felt a few years later with the building of a new set of rooms for Cranmer Hall, including a lecture room, built on the site of the kitchens of number 6, including 'the Barn'.

Cranmer Hall was the first English theological college to admit women students, and no opportunity for buying up premises on the Bailey as they became vacant escaped him – even St Chad's cast-offs [later renamed Linton House]. There were perennial problems of running such an institution on a tight budget. Security, particularly with regard to locking up the premises at night and fire precautions, in the days before the era of Health and Safety regulations, provided a perpetual headache. For its comparatively small numbers, the college punched above its weight with regard to making its presence felt in the wider university activities such as the Union Society, the Students' Union and sporting associations. The undergraduate missions each September were also worthwhile experiences.'

The visionary move to introduce women into Cranmer Hall in 1966 attracted the attention of the local and church press. Rosemary Nixon (Cranmer Hall tutor 1975–89) remembers: 'Jim Hickinbotham had pioneered the joint training of women and men at Cranmer Hall, but the debates about women's ordination were raging in the Church at that time and especially over meals in Cranmer Hall when young men, citing Bible passages, would press their case against the idea. Not until the appointment of Ruth Etchells as principal did the rather clericized, male-dominated feel of the place begin to evaporate.'

The diamond jubilee celebrations marked the climax of Hickinbotham's time in office. A cathedral service marked this in June 1969. The Archbishop of York, Donald Coggan, later Archbishop of Canterbury, preached, and 800 guests were invited to a garden party. Bishop 'R.R.' Williams and Sir James Duff, Lord Lieutenant of County Durham, made speeches reflecting the high

regard in which Hickinbotham was held. (Hickinbotham was subsequently awarded the Lambeth DD.) It was during these celebrations that the building appeal was officially wound up; it included new Cranmer Hall accommodation and a teaching block, a new chapel and gardens behind Cranmer, and the Tristram Room in Bowes House, which was beautified to become, as Hickinbotham put it, 'one of the loveliest 18th-century rooms in Durham'. Numbers at Cranmer Hall had risen to 80, mainly thanks to Hickinbotham's devotion.

Under Hickinbotham St John's College had doubled in size. It was now organized into two halls, had celebrated two jubilees, had seen an ambitious building programme and admitted the first female members of staff and students, who entered Cranmer Hall in 1966.

His successor, John Cockerton, remembers 'how prayerful he was and how he spent time without stint in interviewing candidates and in helping students who consulted him with their problems. Such was the mark of a truly pastoral heart which was evident mainly to those who benefited from it.' After a farewell dinner, Jim and Inge returned to Oxford where he took up the post of principal of Wycliffe Hall. They left behind a much altered and improved college, ready to develop further under the guidance of John Cockerton.

Continuity and Consolidation:
John Cockerton 1970–8

The appointment of John Cockerton as St John's sixth principal showed the college council's desire for continuity and the continuation of the college's broadly evangelical focus. His time as principal was a 'happy time in which things old and new were blended together ... an age of new things in which the values of the old are not forgotten'

— Michael Ramsey in a review of
A College Remembered in *The Churchman*, 1982

John Cockerton arrived in Durham from parish work in St Helens, Lancashire, in January 1958 in a snowstorm in the middle of 'a savage winter'. He remained a staff member for over 20 years. Like Hickinbotham before him, Cockerton read theology at Oxford and trained for ordination at Wycliffe Hall, the daily pattern of which was closely followed by Durham ordinands for at least the first 20 years of Cranmer Hall's existence. He had been a school teacher before beginning ordination training. Cockerton's Anglicanism was firmly evangelical, and, like Wallis, he was a talented musician. He ushered in the new decade by taking up the position of principal in 1970.

Cockerton's aims for the college were four-fold: '(i) to help people to grow into true personhood. St John's is a context in which to develop ... a friendly and accepting and supporting atmosphere ... to allow [students] to grow to personal independence and maturity; (ii) to communicate Christian truth with a view to enlarging people's intellectual appreciation of it and to strengthening their commitment to Christ (staff to influence through patterns in their lives); (iii) to stimulate people to think about world problems. How can a Christian relate constantly to questions facing the world and society immediately around him? (iv) to help students to think about their own calling in the workaday world. This would mean giving attention to their present job – that of a student with academic work to do as well as it can be done and also to future jobs after they go down from the university.'

Principal Cockerton.

Principal's Fact File

- **Principal John P.C. Cockerton**
- Marital status: married Diana Smith in 1975
- Academic expertise: Biblical Theology
- Former positions in college: Greek tutor (1958–60), vice-principal (1968–70), warden (1960–70)
- Bursars: Ralph Kelly, Trevor Pearson, Dennis Sproson
- Warden of Cranmer Hall: Timothy Yates (1971–9)
- Senior Tutors: Robin Nixon, Bruce Kaye
- Vice-Chancellor: Professor Sir Derman Christopherson (1960–79)
- Bishops of Durham: Ian Thomas Ramsey (1966–72), John Habgood (1973–83)

Cockerton was fortunate to develop a strong core team for both halls, making significant changes to the running of St John's and appointing people who retained their connection with the college for many years.

Cockerton was ably assisted in his role as principal by Timothy Yates, who had been a college tutor since 1963 and became warden of Cranmer in 1970, remaining until 1979. Staff numbers significantly increased during this time, as responsibilities diverged and changed as the halls settled into their individual lives. John Gladwin, an Old Johnian from the 1960s, returned to join the staff as tutor in 1971, serving as honorary chaplain to students at St Nicholas's Church, maintaining the good relationships between the college and the 'Church in the Market Place'. He was also one of many former students and staff who rose to the role of bishop (now retired). Susan Brown became the first resident assistant tutor in 1973. She was also instrumental in setting up the Senior Common Room to bring the college into line with other university colleges. Michael Vasey joined as tutor in 1975, so beginning his 23 years on the staff, which was broken by his death in 1998 (see p.50).

David Grieve (1970–4) remembers John Cockerton as 'a lovely, gracious and saintly man who was always there even in the background. Someone you could trust and admire. My year was the first post-Jim, so there was a feeling of loosening up of the previous strictness and a good atmosphere.'

The context into which Cockerton became principal was one of student expansion, both imposed and organic. In 1970 the university set specific targets to increase undergraduate numbers from 3,350 to 5,500 by the end of the decade. This was most obviously achieved through the development of the newly established 'hill' colleges and the amalgamation of the teacher training college of St Hild and the Venerable Bede. Expansion had already gathered momentum at St John's because of the building work, the development of pastoral staff structures and the nurturing of diversity among undergraduates, including women and science students. Significantly, numbers of postgraduates also increased.

It was at this time that the term 'John's Hall' returned to usage: 'An old name, recently brought into use again to designate the larger of the two halls of the college' (Principal's Letter, 1970), this time to both under- and postgraduates in a variety of subjects.

Significant changes to St John's were made in more than name alone. In October 1973 the first female undergraduates were admitted to John's Hall, following the admission of female students to Cranmer Hall in 1966; this is discussed in more detail in the next chapter.

As a constituent college, John's has always had to raise a large part of its own funds in order to survive, and another development

Robin Nixon, first Senior Tutor (1963–75)

Robin Nixon and his family arrived in Durham in 1960 as Cranmer tutor, and in 1963 he became the college's first senior tutor. His main responsibilities related to the administrative demands of the undergraduates, but he also carried out more general duties, including acting as chairman of the college's Development Committee. He thus had unrivalled knowledge of the students, the academic system and the college buildings. He also continued to teach the gospels and liturgy in Cranmer Hall.

Robin oversaw the admission of women undergraduates in 1973, a development of which he was fully supportive.

He left Durham to take up the post of principal of St John's, Nottingham, in September 1975. He died tragicallly in October 1978. John Cockerton paid tribute to him: 'As scholar and teacher, as administrator and unfailing man of ideas, as counsellor and friend, he has been much loved and respected by several generations of Johnians … He was a man of thankfulness and praise. He was always optimistic about the progress of events … His work as pastor was done, first as tutor, then as senior tutor of St John's. He combined a straightforward human interest in people with a deep desire that they should be helped to praise God … He and [his wife] Ruth opened up their home to students and others and gave to their guests simple friendship in a relaxed and happy way. Those who remember his after-dinner speeches at St John's will recall how very amusing he could be … In all the developments which went forward at St John's, Durham, Robin was a key person. A great deal of what was done sprang directly from his ideas and initiatives. He was always thinking of ways in which the college's life could be improved. St John's, it seemed, was forever in his thoughts, despite all the other claims that were made on his time and energy. All this was to the praise of the God he served' (*Robin Nixon: A Life and Tribute*, 1979).

Robin was succeeded by Bruce Kaye.

appeal was launched in 1974 with a target of £125,000. It ran until 1977, raising £71,500, which was boosted by an interest-free loan of £20,000 from the second of St John's significant financial 'saviours', William Leech, and by the provision of wages and materials from the Manpower Services Commission. Alterations were made throughout the college as a result of this fundraising.

Student Numbers

College developments in publicity and building expansion were successful, and numbers climbed steadily from 190 in 1970 to 228 in 1978. The addition of women to both Halls in the 1970s also changed the character of St John's.

Cranmer Hall
1971   62 members (51 men; 11 women)
John's Hall
1974   164 members (129 men; 35 women)

A Johnian remembers

St John's was certainly a vibrant and creative community in the late 1960s and early '70s. I particularly think of the contribution made by people like:

Garth Hewitt, who has devoted his life to mission and to the theme of justice.

Gavin Hewitt (his brother), now one of the most important and effective BBC News Reporters in the world.

Richard Adams, who founded Traidcraft and has spent his life working for justice through trade for the poorest of the world.

St John's has always been an open and welcoming community rooted in Christian faith where people of all cultures and life experiences can flourish in learning for life. Its alumni have made a formidable contribution to both church and society over many generations.

John Gladwin (Cranmer Hall 1966, Tutor 1971–77,
President of College Council 1994–8)

An equally significant move followed this effort in the shape of a Support and Development Fund (which was open for gifts from late 1977). The regular income continued to meet the ongoing basic needs of the college during Cockerton's time, but the idea of the new fund was to make provision for future improvements in buildings, furnishings and so on.

Like Wallis, Cockerton was unmarried when he arrived in Durham, but he surprised the whole college in June 1974 by getting engaged to Diana Smith, a student at Cranmer Hall. Timothy Yates announced the news of their engagement to Cranmer Hall; Robin Nixon (senior tutor 1963–75) announced the news to John's Hall – John and Diana 'went for dinner elsewhere'. Timothy Yates remembers that 'the Cranmer body was so stunned by this that for a long time they seemed unable to come into the common room for coffee!' With a note of unplanned (divine?) humour, the hymn announced at the following morning's chapel service (in the new undergraduate chapel) was 'God moves in a mysterious way, his wonders to perform'. John and Diana were married in Nether Poppleton, York, that August.

Lionel Holmes, who worked on the Development Appeal in 1972–4, remembers: 'John Cockerton … was an extremely easy and delightful person to be working with and we were well matched. The other delightful, but perhaps slightly less easy, character involved at a later stage of the campaign was Lt. Col. Frank Hutchinson. He was very much needed in attracting some of the local bigwigs and did so with precision and panache, devising – inter alia – quite a complicated routine for a reception to be held for them in Cranmer Hall dining room – as being the most suitable venue for such an event (at a time when it was deemed best not to "show off" some of the less presentable parts of the college), complete with a major-domo to announce each guest as they tripped down the step into the dining room. My personal relationship with the Colonel grew very warm, despite the initial hiccups; perhaps I had felt he had come into territory of which I had been too possessive. Certainly we needed all the help we could get. Other members of college staff were very supportive, even though I recall Robin Nixon … suggesting schemes for cramming extra students into

Above: Left to right – Jane Pierssene, Barbara Clayton, David Newsome and Peter Gee, c. 1975.

Left: Principal Cockerton teaching ordinands in mid-70s.

The visit of Her Majesty Queen Elizabeth, Queen Mother on 17 July 1975 with John and Diana Cockerton outside Cruddas House. Her Majesty's visit included a presentation of staff; a visit to Bowes House (no.4); a visit to the Chapel to see the Bowes Hatchment and window. It was 'a very happy day in the history of the College… as far as I know the first royal visit to St John's.' (Principal's letter 1976)

some of the attic areas of the buildings as being decidedly, if delightfully, crackpot.'

Student life developed at its own rate, with a vibrant agenda. Timothy Yates, who was then warden, remembers that 'the period 1970–5 was not easy. We were in the wake of the Paris riots of students of 1968 and even in traditional Durham by 1970 general dissatisfaction with received structures and hierarchies was evident.' Separate JCRs were established for each hall; sporting successes were celebrated; Johnians were heavily involved with student politics (including Adrian Dorber as President of the Students' Union and Richard Blackburn as President of the Union Society); and action was taken on matters of trade justice

in the establishment of the Third World Shop (see p.119).

The Bailey Ball had been established by this time, the 'bops' held in Haughton, and there was increased concern for decibel levels as amplification became louder.

Cockerton's departure in 1978 to take up the post of rector of Wheldrake in the York diocese caused surprise to the college council and to the college as a whole, but he explained in his last letter from St John's to the Old Johnians that after almost 21 years at the college he was ready for a change. The work done under the appeal was completed, the Support and Development Fund had been launched, and a certificate course had been prepared for the coming year. He then fulfilled an ambition to become 'a country parson', asking for and being offered such a parish, some 8 miles southeast of York.

1959: Jubilee Year

A major celebration was held in June 1959 to mark St John's Jubilee year. A thanksgiving service was held in the Cathedral where Michael Ramsey, then Archbishop of York, preached. Mrs Hazel Harrison, wife of the then Chaplain and Bursar, remembers, 'seeing the Head Verger at the Cathedral nearly having apoplexy when Lady Ramsey sat on the top deck in the Choir for the Jubilee Service in 1959. She had sat in the middle row for years'. Later, lunch was held for 550 invited guests in marquees in College gardens. (Sadly, Charles Wallis had died only a few days previously). A toast was made to the newly founded Cranmer Hall, the new venture likened to 'splitting the atom'. This atomic split served St John's as a whole well as it drew in greater numbers (the extensive building work helped the College's capacity), and the student body retained its diversity with married and older ordinands joining the college and often integrating with student activities such as sport and music.

ST. JOHN'S COLLEGE
DURHAM

JUBILEE LUNCHEON

23rd JUNE 1959

There was a real sense of community… central to this being the Christian base of College. There was nothing like that first special year at Durham.

Charlotte South (née Owen) 1973–6

The Introduction of Women:
1966 and 1973

While it was an all-male college St John's was not unusual in its expectations and atmosphere. As a college focused on training Anglican vicars, the tone was of 'gentlemanly scholars' where women were allowed only as visitors for afternoon tea. However, from October 1966 St John's was the first Church of England theological college to train men and women together. Female undergraduates joined the college in October 1973.

Before this date a few members of support staff were female. As early as 1921 the inspectors' report recommended a female housekeeper, although the recommendation was not implemented until 1927. A small number of women lived in Cruddas during the 1940s when St Mary's students were temporarily housed on the Bailey while their new college buildings were finished. Cecily, wife of Principal Williams, and later Inge Hickinbotham, with staff wives, including Hazel Harrison, entertained and offered support to the increasing number of wives and fiancées following the Second World War. Hazel remembers seeing girlfriends at afternoon tea, but they 'had to be gone before Evensong and certainly not seen. Wives did not sleep in college. One character installed a divan for his wife – that project was short lived!' The

attitudes of male staff were still restrained; while she was living in college Hazel was told not to hang out the family's washing as, 'the young men wouldn't like the sight of it'. John Rogan (1946–9, 1952–4) remembers that in the 1950s: 'The Church and the college were obsessed with women. They didn't seem to know how to deal with married ex-servicemen and [those] who had deferred marriage until the end of the war. Married men needed married quarters, and colleges didn't have any. Gradually we edged our way in, but wives were kept beyond the Pale except under strict guard and conditions. One friend had spent years in India, marrying before embarking, but he had never lived with his wife. Nor did he do so in Durham. They met only in vacations.'

Alan Clark remembers St John's in the 1960s: 'Basically, there weren't any women. I think in a Durham colleges' population of about 1,300, fewer than 300 were women. They were protectively ensconced in St Mary's, St Aidan's [St Hild's] and elsewhere on the City's fringes, establishments that were practically off-limits to the majority. I suspect most of us kept rowing and taking cold showers.'

Principal Hickinbotham spearheaded the training of women alongside men at the newly founded Cranmer Hall, having admired women in missionary ministry overseas. The reunion of 'Old Cranmer Hallites' in June 1966 described the process: 'Cranmer Hall has been getting acclimatized to this idea by the ladies being invited in to dinner twice weekly, and this "concession" is to be extended. Masculine exclusiveness is a thing of the past.' Timothy Yates remembers: 'In [October] 1966 another of the principal's visionary ideas took shape, with women coming to train alongside men, then for the post of "parish workers". Some wag had drawn a cartoon of John Cockerton and myself as tonsured monks in the Cranmer "cloister" saying to one another, "all this – and women too". I married Mally Shaw in the college chapel [in 1968] and regard myself as the greatest beneficiary of the experiment which proved its worth on other grounds.'

Chris Edmonson (1968–73) remembers the announcement of the arrival of women students: 'I think it was the warden, Tim Yates, who said to the assembled male gathering, "We will need to learn to embrace the women!"'

Mally Shaw, the women's tutor, was impressed with the 'breadth' of Hickinbotham's vision for St John's College,

Women invaders make history

The Journal, 7th October '66: Mally Yates remembers, 'Those of us who have the privilege of being the first women in what seems to be known widely as the "Cranmer Hall experiment" are very grateful for all that it has given, and is giving, to us.'

Left: In October 1966, eight female students arrived in Cranmer Hall, along with a female tutor, Miss E. Mally Shaw. The students were: Dr Janet Baker; Frances Challen (now Mrs Charles); Jennie Crees; Maisie Jarvis; Sophie Liddell (now Revd Woodhams); Audrey Shilling (Revd); Mary Selwood; Gwen Woolfenden.

particularly the training of women alongside men from October 1966. She had pastoral responsibility for 'the women', in addition to teaching the gospels and Old Testament. The situation, she found 'was all fairly informal. Several of [the women] were older than I was, and we had a strong sense of being thrown together in an unusual situation! Some accommodation had been made available for women in Lightfoot House [now St Chad's]. Others had rooms at the top of Bowes House. In my early months I felt I was being stretched in all directions, but they were made easier by the very supportive attitudes of my colleagues who had all "to a man" been in favour of the admission of women and who were ready to help, advise and share the load. There were minor teething troubles: the Common Room debated at length whether women should be included in the rota for serving at mealtimes until the women tactfully insisted. One or two men were quietly missing if a woman was due to read a service, and the tutor hesitated for a while before she was sure that the ice was broken sufficiently for her to preach in chapel. Men were surprised to find at the beginning of the term that they had a woman tutor to whom they were to read their essays, and some said so, but said it so guilelessly and courteously that she couldn't possibly have taken offence! [Obvious advantages included] the rag concert at the end of the first term found female talent and, of course, a fund of situations on

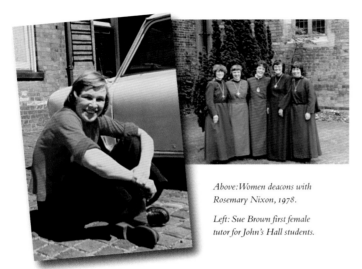

Above: Women deacons with Rosemary Nixon, 1978.

Left: Sue Brown first female tutor for John's Hall students.

which student humour could be let loose … I will long remember with amusement the looks on the faces of the second-year men when, in my first term, I told them that the subject of the weekly seminar I would be taking with them was "The Personal Life of the Clergy" and will remember too with the great courtesy and good humour which they coped with the situation!'

Mally Shaw was succeeded by Ruth Wintle (1969–74) and Rosemary Nixon from 1975.

Other attempts were made to 'integrate' female students, as John Saxbee (1968–72) remembers:'It was during my years at Cranmer that a first attempt was made to have a woman elected as Senior Student. Jean Wadsworth came a close second when we know she had started as a very poor fourth.'

In 1967 Bob Clarke noted in the *Durham Johnian*:'The Hall seems to have taken its Reformation following the introduction of "Les Girls" with calm decorum and distinction. Perhaps their influence may account for a most satisfactory set of exam results.'

JOHN'S HALL, 1973

St John's also blazed a trail in John's Hall, becoming the first male undergraduate college to become mixed in October 1973, both as Cranmer and as John's. Principal John Cockerton remembers that it happened 'very easily, a non-problematic introduction'. Senior tutor, Robin Nixon, oversaw the process and made arrangements for accommodation, and all seemed to go well. In the first year the female students were housed in the top floor of Linton House, the bottom and top of No. 23 North Bailey and three double rooms in the Cottage. Later years led to further integration as women made up half the college.

Jane Grieve (née Piérsénné, 1973–6, later SCR member, staff and ordinand) remembers:'College advertised in the UCCA handbook and sat back to await floods of women applicants. They got me and another girl whose brother was at Cranmer (Helen Stewart).The places were filled by applicants who had anything even vaguely "churchy" in their applications; one girl mentioned her interest in bell-ringing and found her way to John's! The women were housed in groups around the college. Male students nearby were asked to listen out for screams if the women were attacked by marauding locals getting in off the street and to run immediately to our aid!'

Jane's roommate, Helen Stewart (1974–8), also remembers:'I think I was the first female interviewee for St John's Hall. I was applying to read engineering [which only one other Johnian had studied].The information that John's Hall was to admit females was not in the UCCA handbook so that there were very few direct applicants in the first year.Twenty-four hours in the care of John's Hall students [at interview] was enough to convince me that this was where I wanted to be a student. I remember that on the day of my interview a salad lunch had been arranged because the interviewee rep thought that, as a girl, I would prefer that! Male interviewees shared a six-bed dormitory, but I was allocated the principal's guest room … One of the campaigners against the admission of women to John's Hall at this time was my husband to be … I think more girls than anticipated made their grades – girls' accommodation was a bit cramped – I shared what was to have been a ground-floor common room for girls in Number 28 North Bailey – an all-girls enclave complete with resident female tutor, Miss Susan Brown. It was refurbished … As one of the rooms in Linton Wing did not have a "wall-to-wall floor", by comparison these girl's rooms were luxurious with their new furniture and carpets.Those girls in the top of Haughton were less fortunate. During my three years living in, the female enclaves remained; there were no mixed sex corridors.The female/male ratio in college was 23:120; I don't think it mattered to me that there were relatively few girls [the ratio was 6:66 in the Engineering Department].

John's Hall pre-1973

Gillian Boughton, a regular visitor to St John's in the 1970s, later college tutor, remembers John's Hall: 'It was an intoxicating and a completely attractive world, utterly different from the hexagonal modern home where I worked [Trevelyan College]. The sash windows opening onto the Bailey offered glimpses onto a world and a vocabulary which appeared ordered and yet charged with male energy … There were very few women then in Cranmer. Much more common was what D.H. Lawrence described as "the flash of white buttocks" as men chased each other with fire hydrants down corridors.'

David Grieve's graduation, July 1974, with fellow Johnian Jane Piersenne as guest.

'I remember the male students' high level of courtesy. There was a very large number of fire doors between my room and the Haughton dining room, and on one occasion a gentleman fellow student held open every one for me. This was not unusually polite – they always held the doors open for us!

'We always felt the staff really cared about us – did they really pray for us individually at staff meetings?

'Durham University and St John's College are very special places. Three out of four of my children have followed us to Durham, one to St John's.'

An archived 1974 report from the JCR to the college council reflects the contrast between student and staff view of 'the women'. Accommodation was segregated, and students wanted to be integrated, with women treated as equals, not, commented Robert Chalmers, JCR President, 'as women in a

men's college. St John's is now and shall remain a mixed college'. Because of the 'particular tradition and type of student' at St John's, it was argued that the moral risks of mixing students would not be as serious as anticipated.

Charlotte South (née Owen, 1973–6) remembers: 'There was nothing like that first special year at Durham. I think we all felt pretty special and pretty lucky to be in this college. Life at St John's has had a lasting impact on me, and my daughter became a John's girl in 1999. I was delighted then to be able to return and indulge myself on a trip down memory lane!'

In the first year of JCR meetings, female students were made 'honorary gentlemen'. JCR discussions were held throughout 1973–4 to 'put an end to the overt sexism inherent in the title accorded to the Senior Student of this college'. A motion was made to 'abolish the title Senior Man and to restyle the Senior Student President of the JCR' (proposed by R.F. Blackburn, seconded by P. Cunningham), which was eventually carried. There have been five female JCR Presidents since.

It is almost impossible in 2009 to imagine the college without 'John's girls', and now that all Durham colleges are mixed, students' gender is no longer an issue.

St John's College 1974.

Changes, Challenges and Conferences:
Ruth Etchells 1979–88

The appointment in July 1978 of Ruth Etchells as principal was a groundbreaking decision by the college council. Not only a lay person, with a career teaching English rather than theology, she was also a woman, in charge of a college that had became mixed in both halls barely five years earlier (12 years in Cranmer Hall).

As tutor and vice-principal of Trevelyan College between 1968 and 1978 she was well acquainted with the workings and challenges of a Durham college, and she had been a member of the college council since 1973. She took up the post of principal in January 1979, facing a unique set of challenges. Her key aim was to help John's to achieve the standard of other colleges at all levels.

The immediate university context was difficult: increases were demanded in the number of students (to 5,150 between 1976 and 1978) alongside governmental cuts, and colleges therefore needed to demonstrate both academic excellence and value for money. The incoming Vice-Chancellor, Sir Fred Holliday, asked colleges: 'Just what is it that brings us to the top [of student preferences], the total Durham experience?' Etchells aimed for St John's to become the embodiment of this.

As she later wrote:

John's was a small college in a small university far up in the north. It is a danger in any Durham college to turn in on itself. Yet what the college had to offer – to the world! – was a unique and exciting conception; a university hall and a theological college in harness with each other, neither subsuming the other, each preserving its own identity and culture, and yet also sharing a common life to the good of both. The college stood at the junction of the diocese with the wider Church of England community, and beyond that of the worldwide Anglican communion and increasing ecumenical discourse through a good relationship with Ushaw College. It was a natural source of evangelical leadership ... I realized I must encourage staff and students to think across a large canvas, to develop their gifts for those beyond the college as well as within it, to take up, wherever their burdens allowed, tasks in the university, in the wider Church, to participate in the wider deliberations of the times, to be engaged by

the big issues of the world and the Christian community. And I must do the same myself, teaching and preaching and lecturing and debating wherever I was invited and could manage it; 'taking', as Stephen Sykes put it at my 'farewell service', 'the name of the college to parts other colleges could not reach'. Somehow, that is, embodying the thrilling vision which was at the very heart of this college.

Right: The stained glass panel, 'Prodigal Love', was donated by Principal Etchells and now hangs in Leech Hall.

Article in church newspaper CWN Series, June 1983: an interview with Ruth Etchells as Principal of St John's College with Cranmer Hall.

The outgoing Vice-Chancellor, Sir Derman Christopherson, was frank with Etchells about the 'precarious' nature of the university's accreditation of St John's in its current academic standing. The admissions procedure and culture of academic expectation within St John's needed 'urgent and radical work'. The perception of college, both internally and externally, needed to be challenged. The Vice-Chancellor noted that: 'unquestionably, preference was given in admissions there to the Christian applicant who was barely qualified academically, rather than the able applicant who was not a Christian but was willing to accept the Christian ethos of the Hall.' Etchells remembers that: 'The government was pressing the universities towards a more balanced composition of arts, social sciences and sciences. Yet 80 per cent of John's Hall students were currently reading for degrees in arts or social science, preponderantly in theology, or – a now abolished course – "the general arts degree", which often lacked credibility in the university. This image of St John's had to be dispelled. For me a Christian university college was by definition one which demanded the very highest academic integrity, one which recognized that the first purpose of a university education was academic, and that a Christian university education meant bringing all one's intellectual faculties and assumptions to the scrutiny of one's faith.

'Two things followed: first, that students must be challenged to achieve the highest possible standard of which each individual was capable, and they must be admitted on the basis of real academic potential for this, while accepting the hall's Christian basis. Second, that they must also be challenged to relate their studies to their Christian faith were they believers, and be presented with the challenge of the Christian faith – not least to their intellects! – where they were not. I believed then, and still

The Winter of 1979

'As I write, the grubby remains of the snow heaps around our buildings and along the Bailey still mark what has been one of the worst winters here in Durham within anyone's memory … The domestic and administrative staff have gallantly battled through blizzards to reach us, though on two separate occasions they were unable to get through because of waist-high drifts. We fared not too badly during all the food shortages, thanks primarily to heroic efforts by our catering officer, Max; though for a brief period we ran short of such necessities as sugar. Both among students and staff, there was a period when practically everyone was either just recovering from 'flu or about to succumb to it! What is remarkable, and tremendously reassuring, has been the buoyancy of the whole college community in the midst of all these disasters. Nothing could have been warmer than the welcome they have given me, or the atmosphere of the college community as a whole. As all Johnians know better than I do, it clearly takes more than a bit of bad weather to chill that'

Principal's Letter, 1979

believe, that a vitally important part of the college's engagement in 'mission' was in the quality of life and thought that it could present to its non-Christian members and their friends from outside. I realized that the student balance across the faculties must be changed urgently; for reasons educational as political. I was greatly blessed here in finding myself working with a senior tutor, Dr Bruce Kaye, who had long perceived the desirability of such a change in the admissions style of the college, and who worked devotedly with me to achieve it.'

And so the intake for October 1979 arrived, 'better qualified and presenting a wider subject range, including significantly more scientists and mathematicians, the fruits of which were seen in

Staff Memories

Christopher Byworth (warden 1979–83) writes: 'My enduring memory was of belonging to a close-knit, caring Christian community, which included friends from outside the hall as well as staff and students within it. Ruth Etchells as principal and Ken Kitchin, the bursar, were particularly outstanding colleagues to work with. The emphasis was on ever-greater excellence in the academic field and in the quality of our buildings. Reorganizing timetables and constant meetings with every group represented ate up time and produced minutes galore but also usually goodwill and the acceptance of change.'

Margaret Masson (resident tutor 1983–6, senior tutor 1992–99) remembers: 'I first arrived at John's in the spring of 1982 to be interviewed for a resident tutorship. I was intrigued by the world of St John's from the start: immediately striking was the friendliness and warmth of all the people, and I was impressed by the way the staff took very seriously the college's identity as a Christian college within the university. This, more than anything, made me want to be a part of this place and has continued to inspire me about St John's. Ruth Etchells was also a major inspiration. I wanted to work with her for my PhD, and it was a real privilege having her as both principal and supervisor. She was a hugely influential figure in those formative years – to me and to countless others! Saying yes to her then (and I can still clearly remember her gaze in that moment) felt like one of the decisive, fateful, providential moments in my life – and I have never regretted it!

Staff photo 1979 College officers: Byworth, Kitchin, Etchells, Kaye. Etchells' appointment as Principal coincided with a number of new appointments: 'God gave a new team at the right time' including Ken Kitchen as new Bursar; Principal's Secretary, 'the wonderful Doris Kay, I was so blessed'; Christopher Byworth as Warden in 1979 and Bruce Kaye as Senior Tutor. The tradition of College officers' Monday morning meeting continued, to 'hear each others' diaries' and concerns, offer up items and students for prayer.

'I was also captivated by the beauty of Durham on that first visit. I remember taking a walk that evening up to Palace Green: the cathedral and the Celtic cross outside wonderfully illuminated. The magic of the place – city and college – made me know, like so many others, that I wanted to be a part of this. For three years, I lived in John's as a resident tutor. This proved very useful experience when I returned later as senior tutor. I already knew almost every nook and cranny of the place and although a young and inexperienced senior tutor at the start, in some areas at least, it was hard to pull the wool over my eyes. For two of those years I shared a flat with Gill Boughton and there started a wonderful, sustaining friendship. At the start of our flat-sharing, I was a little daunted by Gill: she was older, an experienced professional woman newly returned from the exotic Far East, incredibly English (to my Scottish sensibilities!), who intimately knew this Durham world, which was, to me, a mystery that needed not a little decoding. She turned out to be an immensely kind mentor and friend, and it has been intriguing to see how intertwined our lives have remained over the years!

'Those years of being a resident tutor in John's were very formative. There was a wonderful group of young resident tutors, including the Trebilcos, the Gohs, the Langfords, who were all friends, and I was grateful for the community that made the PhD years much, much less isolating than they were for some of my contemporaries. In particular, I have fond memories of Steve Langford's d-j evenings in their tiny and pretty un-soundproofable flat at the end of Linton Wing. Steve had the most amazing collection of singles, and we would sometimes get together and

Left: Staff photo 1985: 'When we look at some of the people serving as tutors or college officers during these years, the reason for the college's development in excellence becomes clear.' Etchells 2005. A few long-serving staff members can be spotted here, including Margaret Masson, Gillian Boughton, Douglas Davies, Michael Vasey, Pauline Williams, Faye Slinn, Ted Tait and Martin Clemmett.

Bottom: The arrival of the Queen Mother, greeted by Principal Etchells and a array of umbrellas on the Bailey, at the opening of Leech Hall in 1987.

choose singles we wanted him to play: wonderful evenings of music and nostalgia!

'Peter Forster was senior tutor. He was fun and had a sense of mischief and philosophical pragmatism that served his role well. On more than one occasion, his recipe for young troubled female students was that they find a man! Fortunately, not said, as far as I know, to their face!

'I became friends with Michael Vasey in those years. He was very kind to me in my early days at John's, aware, I think, of how new and strange it all was for me. His gentleness and kindness to me then – a young outsider – meant a great deal.'

Ian Cundy (warden from 1983) remembers that there was a great sense that Ruth Etchells was a trailblazer as the first lay female principal of a theological college. Ian fondly remembers their close working relationship at this time. She was very 'hands on' with students on both sides of college; for example, both he and she signed the reports to the diocesan bishops on each ordinand during their training (later principals have not been so involved). Ian describes this as a 'shared ministry' between the two senior figures.

Peter Forster (senior tutor and tutor in Church history and Christian doctrine), remembers that Ruth Etchells had a 'very personal interest in her college and made it her business to know all her students, from both sides'. The team was a strong unit. They 'worked hard but relaxed hard, enjoying each other's company. Ruth made sure we did.'

June three years later, when our degree results for 1982 were really commendable. The academic quality of our admissions never looked back from then on. Successive senior tutors, Peter Forster and Margaret Masson, followed the same astringent policy. The college began to be known as one you had to work to get into.' By November 1982 five applicants named John's as their first choice for every place available. 'Bruce Kaye had done a marvellous job, as did his successors … The climax of all this was in 1987, when coinciding with the Queen Mother's visit to open Leech Hall, and the college looking simply resplendent, the degree results across both halls were the finest in the college's history, truly outstanding. By then John's had become a regular contender for first place in the unofficial league table among the colleges.'

Challenges remained: 'The college was seriously under-funded and had been so for some time. By 1978 all the other Durham colleges were of necessity supplementing their income by major vacation trade. Our poor facilities meant we had few areas where we could offer suitable conference accommodation. Since this was, financially speaking, the lifeblood of the other colleges, and – to continue the metaphor – we were dying of financial anaemia without injections of it – this was a very serious difficulty indeed.' The increase of conference trade was a major catalyst in the improvement of college facilities in

Etchells's early years. 'There is no doubt at all that under the guidance of the dedicated bursar, Ken Kitchin, and Martin Clemmett's tireless work as steward from 1980 and skilled leadership of the domestic staff who serviced the conferences, together with their unshakeable kindness and good humour, won for us trade which our facilities would otherwise have lost. From 1981 we were greatly helped by the contract with the Open University, 100 students at a time for nine weeks in the summer. It was not until we had upgraded the whole place in 1997–8 that the conference trade became truly competitive and I believe has remained so ever since.'

Etchells's aim was to 'make the place glorious for God'. When Professor Fred Holliday joined the university in 1980 as Vice-Chancellor he stayed for a term in each of several colleges. The state of the buildings and furnishings was a 'severe handicap', and his strictures had the more force because he had put his foot through the rotting floorboards of the corridor outside his room only a week earlier. The most obvious realization of this was ultimately the building of the William Leech Hall, but first came the refurbishment of all college bedrooms and the installation of wash basins in all rooms: 'Increasingly, students and the university expected colleges to provide well-kept accommodation with pleasant public rooms and amenities, high academic standards, financial solvency,

Archbishop Robert Runcie and his chaplain, Ruth Etchells in the Great Hall of the People, Beijing, being presented to Madame Chow. Throughout 1983 in particular, Principal Etchells travelled internationally on the college's behalf with the aim of 'taking the college to the world, and the world to the college.' Other places visited included teaching at the world's most northerly theological college in the Arctic and acting as Anglican representative on the World Council of Churches.

smooth and effective administration, reliable and sensitive tutorial care, and a good community ethos. John's was splendid on the two latter; but way behind most other colleges on the rest. I shall not easily forget my interviews in those early days with the distraught and angry parents of some women freshers, appalled by the beds on bricks, army blankets and soiled ticking

Anthem: Easter St John

God so loved he gave
God loved so he gave
God loved, he gave so
So teach me to love
So I may love, I'll give
So I may give, I'll love
I may so love to give.
Teach me Lord to give,
And loving give and giving love,
So Thou be gift and love so.
Words Ruth Etchells, tune Philip Munch.

Right: Staff and friends' reunion at the college's 70th anniversary, 1979.

Laughter, enquiring minds, a sincere interest in life, a balanced perspective, enjoyment of things that enrich life, and awareness of the deep things – these are the common threads. The connections and shared values continue. We continue to look ahead, and to live.
Richard Horton 1983–6

pillows of the bedrooms their cherished daughters were about to dwell in. I wholly agreed with their indignation!'

Beds and bedding were updated, utility rooms were improved (particularly in Cruddas), and the Linton and Bailey Rooms were refurbished.

The university's jubilee in 1985 was a great occasion for college to celebrate its journey so far. Robert Runcie, Archbishop of Canterbury, was invited to the college for lunch and a tour, the beginning of a close friendship with college. Etchells remembers showing the Johnian spirit, 'generous, admiring, hospitable'.

A second 'great lunch' was held in honour of Margot Fonteyn's installation as the new chancellor in 1983.

Of course, a college is more than its buildings and reputation. 'This cherished little college' was charged above all with 'bringing on students', which was 'just a joy'. As far as possible, Etchells held an 'open door' policy for students, in which she was helped by both her personal assistants, Doris Kay and Doreen Ayling, who had children of university age. She was also assisted by JCR presidents. Students were involved with activities including the college orchestra, two choirs, the Pastoralia scheme throughout Durham county, Northern Ireland Youth Encounter, the Third World Shop and fundraising for the developing world (such as the Third World Walk from Durham to London). College teams celebrated success in volleyball, football, hockey and men's rugby. The boat club was experiencing something of a revival at this time, and a new restricted four was purchased. Two senior ladies' crews rowed and one boat was sent to the Head of the River Race on the Thames for the first time in history.

In March 1988 Etchells's farewell service was held in Durham Cathedral with the Archbishop of York presiding; Stephen Sykes, the president of the college council, preached, and around 600 guests were entertained in college. Etchells was awarded the Lambeth DD for services to the Church by Archbishop George Carey in 1992 and received an Honorary DLitt by her own University of Liverpool in 2003. She has continued to publish collections of personal prayers alongside texts on praying with English poets and studies in contemporary literature. In addition, she wrote the archbishop's Lent book for 1995, *Set My People Free*, and *A Reading of the Parables of Jesus* (1998). Although she is now retired, she remains affectionately concerned for the college and was delighted that her stained glass panel, 'Prodigal Love', was accepted for Leech Hall.

Above: Principals past, present and future: Anthony Thiselton, Ruth Etchells and Stephen Sykes at Lambeth Palace at the conferment of Etchells' Doctorate in Divinity, June 1992.

Left: In June 1984, Dame Margot Fonteyn visited St John's as part of the University's 150th anniversary celebrations, starting her time as Chancellor. The College choir sang in the Linton hallway. Principal Etchells remembers this occasion epitomising the dedication to St John's shown by both staff and students at this time.

Planning and Progress:
Anthony Thiselton 1988–92

Formerly senior lecturer in biblical studies in the University of Sheffield, Anthony Thiselton had also been principal of St John's namesake in Nottingham. He served on the Church of England Doctrine Commission and was advisory editor of the *Journal for the Study of the New Testament*. He had experience of parochial ministry in urban, suburban and rural churches and was once visiting professor in the USA and Canada. In a prospectus from the 1980s he listed his interests as 'a Cavalier King Charles dog and choral and organ music'.

Tony Thiselton arrived as principal in April 1988. He admits that his previous knowledge of St John's came from Professor James Atkinson, professor of biblical studies at Sheffield (member of the college council and undergraduate 1933–7), where Thiselton was senior lecturer. According to a 1980s prospectus, Thiselton was clear about the unique nature of St John's College: 'Our college's uniqueness arises partly from its two-fold character. It remains a constituent college of the university and also an evangelical Christian foundation. St John's College currently consists of some 22 tutorial staff (plus support staff) and over 300 students (11 teaching staff and up to 80 ordinands from Cranmer Hall). The shared resources of the college thus offer a richer and

more varied range of facilities and opportunities than are available in most other {theological} colleges … We are not simply part of a privileged intellectual world. The university context nourishes intellectual enquiry, honesty and debate; our context in the northeast maintains an awareness of economic and spiritual need.'

Thiselton remembers: 'I was blessed at St John's with two wonderful personal assistants. First, Doreen Ayling was magnificent. I recall her helping fit 6,000 books into my study and the adjacent hall. One day the bishop's council was to be held in the Tristram Room. Everything was arranged perfectly. But in our absence students plundered the flowers and much decorative material. Mrs Ayling, however, checked the room at about 6.30 am and guessed who were the chief culprits. She knocked them awake and by 8.45 the room looked its original perfect form. I knew nothing about this until Monday morning. When Mrs Ayling left, I was devastated. Could I do the job without a brilliant and devoted PA? In the event Aileen Jones stepped into the breach [from June 1999]. She had not only been Peter Forster's secretary, but had once served as secretary to the university registrar. She knew all the university secretaries, and was brilliant at letting me know what was going on behind the scenes. Like Doreen Ayling, she was deeply caring both for the college and for me.'

The symbolic handover between Principal Etchells and Principal Thiselton, 1988.

Similarly, Thiselton was well served by his bursar, John Hirst, who 'has been tireless in his utter commitment and outstanding administrative gifts, combining meticulous care of fabric and finance with pro-active planning and sensitive Christian vision' (Principal's Letter, 1992).

Following his predecessor's tradition, Thiselton admits that much of his time was spent teaching in Cranmer Hall, which by this time included the Wesley Study Centre (opened in 1988) and was working with Cranmer's warden, Ian Cundy, to develop a new degree in theology and ministry, validated in 1991.

Expansion was encouraged in the university's strategy document, *Durham 2000*, which proposed a phased expansion from 6,000 students to 7,500 by the year 2000, which placed 'considerable strain on college accommodation, including bed spaces, public rooms and management structures. St John's College recognized the need to preserve the intimacy and sense of community that characterizes its ethos of care for others; but we have no intention of opting out of our responsibilities to the rest of the university' (Principal's Letter, 1992).

Building alterations continued with the complete refurbishment of the kitchens in the summer of 1991. 'Astute financial management meant that the costings of £70,000 were met. The Bailey Room was refurbished for use as the Junior Common Room in term time. The grounds gained a new look, thanks largely to the initiative, time and hard work of Mrs Fuller and to donations from the St John's Society.' The chapel underwent a period of 'new vitality and diversity, which has characterized chapel services, without sacrificing liturgical tradition, propriety and dignity'.

In 1987 the Enterprise in Higher Education Initiative was launched by the government to assist higher education institutes to develop enterprising graduates in partnership with employers. Durham was one of the first universities to be granted five years of funding (1988–93) to pursue this aim through the Enterprise Bureau. St John's, under the guidance of Jane Grieve, was one of the first colleges to get involved, primarily by coordinating and hosting 'value added' courses, first open to students in the five Bailey colleges, then throughout the university. Courses included language skills, computer literacy, preparation for employment and personal development. A total of 279 students registered in the first two terms of 1991–2. This scheme developed into Training for Success, which ran until the summer of 2000. A succession of Johnians facilitated a series of 'value-added' courses,

'The Lithograph', a collection of students' reflections on college life, was published throughout the 1980s–90s.

ranging from British Sign Language to essay-writing skills, beginners' Russian to Spanish. Sadly, due to lack of continued funding, the increase in similar courses university-wide and the provision of modular, interdepartmental degree courses, TFS's final courses were hosted in 2000–1, under Amabel Craig as coordinator, following in the footsteps of Vicky Cooke, David Davies, Miles Huckle, Claire Firth, Gillian Boughton and Jane Grieve.

Helen Bartlett, who has been involved with the college since 1988, remembers Thiselton: 'I always felt as if I needed to look after him and yet he was an eminent and forceful academic, a force to be reckoned with!'

Thiselton was well liked and respected among the undergraduates. Adrian Vincent (1990–3) remembers: 'Professor Thiselton was the quintessential academic. Some of us referred to him, behind his back, as "Tone Loc", the black American rap artist who had recently had the hit "Funky Cold Medina" and who bore not the slightest resemblance to Prof. Thiselton in any way.'

Thiselton, in turn, 'was proud of our St John's students when the other colleges went on rent strike. I showed our exec the books and asked whether they preferred less heating, poorer food or wished to deprive our good ladies of some wages when often they were the only earner in the family. In the event St John's was the only college not to go on rent strike. The exec informed the student body that we were doing our best.' Adrian Vincent remembers: 'It was not Professor Thiselton's argument at the meeting about the rent strike that persuaded most not to join it, but the fact that Professor Thiselton was such a kindly, unworldly man, no one wanted to go on strike in case it upset him. As one of the two St John's students who joined the rent strike I was later very grateful to Professor Thiselton, because when the strike was over and it came to paying my rent arrears, the college bursar was keen to charge me a punitive rate of interest. Professor Thiselton called me into his study with the bursar, asked whether

I had gone on the rent strike out of principle or in order to save money. When I said it was out of principle, he told the bursar I was not to be charged a punitive rate and he checked with me that I could manage the repayments.'

In the Principal's Letter of 1992 he wrote: 'I could continue about how we regularly won the competition with boats, or how we gained eight first class degrees in theology during my last year as principal, or how we began the university carol service. But my space is limited. The other occasion that made me most proud of St John's was when there had been strife between the college and mid-youth of the city. The Vice-Chancellor of the university requested that all principals would provide a list of activities that the college arranged for the city. St John's provided a list as long as your arm, but none was forthcoming from any of the other colleges. Our prison visiting, our providing holidays for deprived children and so on, makes St John's college distinctively a college with a Christian ethos. The stable core of the college's corporate identity lies in the character and the hearts of Johnians. Like a living human being, the identity of the college grows and develops, in order to attain fresh stature and maturity. As the years pass, some external features change; the college retains the same corporate entity, rooted in its history, in the purpose of its foundation, and in its explicitly Christian and evangelical tradition.

Thiselton's short time as principal can be summarized in two words: planning and progress. He remembers: 'The four college officers – Ian Cundy, Peter Forster, John Hirst and I, plus latterly Margaret Masson – spent hours on various plans for a second site. About three were aborted as unsuitable, and then began the work of planning the old hospital site. I came to the opening. We also spent much time on satisfying the conflicting demands of the University Safety Officer and the Conservation Officer on new fire doors, which had to be custom made, and refurbishing Linton and other properties. John Hirst recovered £7,000 on estimated gas readings that [had been] overcharged! We also needed to appoint a new catering manager, and raise more funds. Then we planned the Cranmer degree in theology and ministry done two-thirds in the college and one-third in the university.

'As for academic and other success, we were second in demand to Castle (sometimes third after Collingwood); I was made Honorary Professor of Theology and wrote *New Horizons in Hermeneutics* (700 pages); we gained eight firsts in theology and were written up in *Cosmopolitan* as the best place to go for theology: other subjects did very well in degrees; we were head of the river; and the orchestra was impressive. I always kept an eye on musical ability when considering admissions. Later "expansion" came in the wake of all this!'

Communication and Continuing Confidence:
David Day 1992–9

'St John's has never just been a place for serious study, however. The life of the spirit, by which in this instance I mean the human spirit, has always flourished alongside workouts on one's intellectual muscles. I have always wanted the college to be a place of imagination, creativity and, please God, laughter. I now suspect that if you give the members of this community enough space and back their daft schemes with money, then the creativity will look after itself'

Principal Day, College Record, 1999

Principal's Fact File

- **Principal David Vivian Day**
- Marital status: married to Rosemary; 3 children
- Academic background: Education, Theology
- Major books published: *This Jesus, Teenage Beliefs, Beyond the Here and Now ..., The Preaching Workbook*
- Senior Tutors: Margaret Masson, Gill Boughton
- Chaplains: Mark Cartledge (1997–03)
- Wardens: John Pritchard, Stephen Croft
- Vice-Chancellor: Professor Evelyn Ebsworth (1990–9)
- Bishops of Durham: David Jenkins (1984–94), Michael Turnbull (from 1994)

After a short interregnum David Day was installed as the ninth principal of St John's in January 1993. In his inaugural speech in Durham Cathedral he referred to his vision for St

Principal Day.

John's as a meeting place for Christian faith and secular culture, in addition to the development of Cranmer Hall's teaching of preaching and communicating the gospel: 'At St John's we are committed to an idea of education generously and liberally conceived ... We try to provide opportunities for young adults to grow. We try to preserve the niceties and traditional formalities of civilized living. We try to encourage risk-taking and the acceptance of responsibility. Complacent or not, I believe we have something infinitely precious here – and something very fragile' (*College Record*, 1997).

In his installation speech Day said: 'Previous principals have been licensed – which does have a pleasantly alcoholic flavour about it ... I'll settle for installed. Central heating is supposed to go everywhere and be everywhere, not to be excessively noisy in operation and keep everyone warm and content. Not a bad job description for a principal' (*College Record*, 1999).

Day had been invited by Ruth Etchells to join the SCR and college council in the late 1980s, in addition to giving a few Cranmer lectures on Christian education and sermons in the college chapel. Day had 14 years' teaching experience in secondary schools, became head of religious education, then senior lecturer at Bishop Lonsdale College, Derby, and latterly senior lecturer at Durham School of Education.

The existing university context reflected increasing governmental concern to expand access to higher education, and

Michael Vasey, Liturgy Tutor (1975–98)

A much loved and valued member of the college, Michael Vasey was tutor in liturgy from 1975.

Ian Bunting (director of pastoral studies 1971–8) remembers: 'It was a miracle that he was ever appointed in the first place. I still remember the interview when it seemed that his first answer to every question from the staff was, "I don't know." The principal and warden perceived, as I came to do, that he was someone who loved the Church passionately, if also angrily.'

Christopher Byworth (warden 1979–83) remembers Michael having 'a fresh and profound mind on the Alternative Service Book'. Ian Cundy (warden 1983–92), remembers him as an 'extraordinary, very able, fascinating person who wouldn't like to lose an argument. He had the sharpest mind which could be both unnerving and disarming. He had the capacity to sum up a person's character in a sentence; he was both brilliant and devastating, such a series of contradictions. We were all very fond of him. Michael maintained very close contact with many former students.'

John Pritchard (warden 1993–6), recalls: 'Michael was a fascinating colleague, warm, witty, sharp, infuriating and, above all, principled on various matters about which he felt passionately. On the issue of gay people and the Church, Michael was prepared to walk straight into the line of fire. He was shot many times.'

James Stewart (Cranmer 1997–2000) remembers him as his 'beloved tutor, mentor and surrogate father-figure'.

In 2000, a year after Michael's death his ashes were interred on the south side of the chapel.

Controversy began when Michael's book, *Strangers and Friends*, was published on 6 December 1996. It was an exploration of homosexuality and the Bible. Day, along with the warden, John Pritchard, wrote a letter to the Church Press describing the book as, 'on any reckoning a work of scholarship, which employs insights from sociology and history to redraw the map of the debate about the Christian attitude to homosexuality. It is a book full of subtleties and at times very moving in its portrayal of the contemporary gay experience and always concerned to give proper weight to the biblical witness and to the varieties of teaching which together make up the Christian tradition.' At the same time, two other Cranmer tutors, Mark Bonnington (New Testament) and Bob Fyall (Old Testament), co-authored a Grove Booklet on homosexuality and the Bible, articulating, expounding and defending the historic position of the Church on 'the gay issue'.

Margaret Masson remembers: 'There [were] difficult times – one was the difficult and painful era surrounding the homosexuality debate when David had the very lonely and personally costly job of holding us all together as a staff and as a college. That he largely did so is a mark of his leadership skills and the respect in which we all hold him.'

Michael's untimely death in 1998 was felt by the whole college and the Anglican Church. Margaret Masson remembers him as: 'A one off [who made] such an impression on so many. He was wonderful at seeing things that others may have passed by and giving them the confidence to believe in certain gifts themselves, a great encourager. More than possibly anyone else I have known, he made me rethink my ideas and prejudices. I miss the chance to chew things over with him and be challenged and possibly changed by the unexpected vistas he would open up!

'He was, of course, sometimes impossible. ("Moi?" I can see him shrug his shoulders and look quizzically innocent.) He would never concede anything for a quieter life.

'The deterioration in his health and rapid weight loss towards the end was painful to watch. Especially as he still was able to muster what strength he had for some amazing feats of preaching. That made the suddenness of his death all the more shocking: how could the man who had preached so brilliantly the previous Tuesday now be dead just a few days later? His funeral in Durham Cathedral was both a terribly sad and yet beautiful occasion – much of it had been planned by Michael. The finale – Edith Piaf's "Je ne regrette rien" bursting out over the cathedral's PA system just when everyone thought the service was over was a marvellous and a wonderfully Michael touch and it was a remarkable moment of drama – sharing in the tears turning to laughter. But it was some years before I could listen to that song again!'.

Laying the foundation stone of St Margaret's Garth student accommodation in September 1996: Senior Tutor Margaret Masson and Principal David Day.

the university was under pressure to offer more places. (In 1990 there were 4,716 undergraduates at Durham, scheduled to rise to 7,535 in 1999.) St John's physically expanded to keep up with this demand. In 2000 the college community totalled 500, a figure that had doubled in only 20 years. Day puts this down to both the current climate of fully grant-maintained undergraduates in addition to 'an amazing team' and the 'wise stewardship of college bursars', John Hirst and Robert Scott-Biggs.

Day put much energy and effort into the college buildings, both on the Bailey site and, most significantly, developing St Margaret's Garth: student accommodation in the centre of Durham for both undergraduates and Cranmer families. Day's particular concern was to ensure that undergraduates were 'not thrown on the mercy of Durham landlords' then known to raise their rents for student lettings. The Garth also included the Crossgate Centre as a business letting and the Centre for Christian Communication. Day remembers that the role of council members such as John Norris, Nigel Sherlock and Roger Kingdon was invaluable.

Johnians' involvement throughout the university and in schemes of wider social involvement, such as the Northern Ireland Youth Encounter, Third World Shop and local

parochial involvement, was becoming well known. As Day comments in his final principal's report: 'I have always wanted the college to be a place of imagination, creativity and, please God, laughter. I now suspect that if you give the members of this community enough space and back their daft schemes with money, then the creativity will look after itself.'

Reflecting his concern for alumni to retain their connection with St John's current crop of students, Day instituted Five Years On dinners, inviting all leavers to return after five years, bringing £100 with them as a donation to the Student Hardship Fund. The first Leavers' Dinner was held in July 1998 and continues.

A new college flag was bought for the opening of the Crossgate Centre on 28 Feburary 1997, with the assistance of St John's Society and an ex-professional flag-maker at Cranmer Hall. Georgina Wilczek (née Luck) remembers: 'The college flag … disappeared for about three days and its disappearance caused quite a furore. I believe it turned up in the JCR flat (Yusef [Khan] was JCR President at the time)! Once handed back, the flag was re-hung on top of Haughton instead.'

Ceri Huws wrote: 'Its eventual and celebrated return to the principal's office restored his confidence in student and humankind and each of us who had seen the flag in its glory and splendour breathed a sigh of relief. The rampant lion and golden eagle live on' (*College Record*, 1997).

Day admits that he 'loved the undergraduates', and he was, in turn, popular with them. The range of student activities, concerns and achievement that flourished under his leadership is reflected in his final principal's report:

'We want the college to be a place where concern for scholarship is encouraged and not disparaged … So this year we won the Durham intercollegiate *University Challenge* shield and

First Class Honours Degrees

The college's academic success through the 1990s was shown by increasing numbers of first class degrees.

1991–15; 1992–12; 1993–14; 1994–10; 1995–14; 1996–10;
1997–14; 1998–17; 1999–18;

Cranmer Hall teaching sessions at the Centre for Christian Communication in the Cross Gate Centre.

The Centre for Christian Communication (1996–2005)

The 'CCC' sought to challenge the Church nationally to take more seriously the training given to ministers and readers in preaching apologetics and media skills in the 21st century. Based in the Cross Gate Centre, it included offices, conference rooms and multi-media studio which proved popular with college musicians and aspiring bands. As well as providing courses and facilities for the students at Cranmer and the Wesley Study Centre, the centre organized regional training days, consultations and national conferences, such as the annual Durham Preaching Conference, in addition to a major four year research and training project, VOX.

As director from 1996, I oversaw the configuration and equipping of the Centre's facilities and was joined in 1999 by David Wilkinson as associate director and fellow in Christian Apologetics. The centre was made possible by generous start-up grants and seed funding from the Jerusalem Trust and the William Leech Trust, and significant support from the Garfield Weston Foundation, Sir Halley Stewart Trust, as well as the St Margaret's Church Estate Charity. The work at the CCC also prospered through the dedication of many individuals – paid and unpaid, student and staff – who gave of their time and energy to bringing a vision to reality.

The centre closed in 2005, when the college was unable to secure further funding for it, with the commission that the need to train church leaders who are able to communicate effectively in a visually oriented, media-dominated society remains as great as ever. I believe we have succeeded in raising awareness of this critical shortfall in the church's training provision.

Geoffrey Stevenson, former Director

---

two of the winning team will represent Durham in the televised version, Paxman and all. So many John's students were commended at Union debates that we instituted a public speaking competition. Members of John's, Cranmer and the staff contested the issue fiercely. The prize went to James Stewart for a witty and erudite speech on "Sex is all right but it will never replace the bicycle". Two freshers thought they would start a croquet competition. Coastal Dune, our own rock group, cut a CD and saw it on sale in Our Price. The orchestra and choir put on termly concerts of a very high standard, Camerata reproduced on disc their own distinctive brand of beautifully controlled, polyphonic, unaccompanied choral singing, and Bare Witness maintained the college's dramatic reputation. Jane Speck and Rebecca Stonehill won Bowron Bursary Awards to go and work for the relief of poverty in India, Kuhan Satkunanayagam was elected President of the Durham Union Society, and Phil Melia served as president of DULOG, following in the footsteps of a John's tutor of 20 years ago. With an impressive grasp of priorities, Tara Duncan turned down a modelling contract in order to study for a higher degree in compost, thus earning herself a full-page photo in the *Daily Mail* under the headline "Manure Student". Well done Tara, you shine like a beacon in a naughty world.'

Margaret Masson described Day as 'a passionate, articulate, behind-the-scenes advocate and conscience – whether for individuals or structures' (*College Record*, 2000). At his departure the JCR and CCR Presidents put together a video of a college-wide tribute to David, a rendition by different groups of amended lyrics of the Lou Reed song 'Perfect Day' (then used in BBC advertising), recorded by the choir and orchestra at the Centre for Christian Communication. Different groups were filmed, singing parts of the soundtrack in a number of venues, covering as wide a range of staff and student interests as possible involving over 100 members of college: John's and Cranmer tutors and execs, bursarial, cleaning and cooking staff, the maintenance team and development campaign, the rugby and football teams, choir and orchestra: 'Oh, what a David Day!'

Day left St John's to train for ordination and is assistant curate at St Nicholas's Church in Durham's marketplace.

'The question that is uppermost in my mind is, "Have we, in the last seven years, kept faith with those who founded the college and those who have lived in it for the last 90 years?" I hope so. When I started as principal I was overawed by the line of principals from Nowell Rostron to Tony Thiselton who stared at me from the walls of the SCR. We have now reframed, resized and, in most cases, magnified their faces, and they hang alongside the main staircase. As I go home I look at the one at the top who twinkles at me conspiratorially. Halfway down I come to a principal who is recorded as describing the then Professor of Theology (who shall be nameless) as "that complete lunatic … I have just watched him walking down the Bailey with one foot on the pavement and the other in the gutter." By now you will have guessed that this must be Charles Wallis. He stares at me with gimlet eyes, and I look the other way as he whispers "pantomimes indeed". At the bottom of the stairs the formidable Dawson Dawson-Walker hisses, "Consider the possibility that you have been placed on this earth to be a dreadful warning to others." I turn the corner, open the great doors and slip into the Bailey.'

Into the New Millennium:
Stephen Sykes 1999–2006

The Rt Revd Professor Stephen Sykes was appointed tenth principal at the dawn of the new millennium. His previous involvement with St John's as president of the college council (1984–94) meant that he was familiar with the college's unique nature, was sympathetic to its ethos and had already begun some of the work he was to continue as principal. His first connection with St John's was while he was Van Mildert Canon Professor of Divinity (1974–85), when he had been invited to SCR events. He was also a colleague of Anthony Thiselton for a short time. Immediately before his appointment as principal, he was Bishop of Ely (1990–9), Regius Professor of Divinity at Cambridge University and chair of the Church of England's Doctrine Commission from 1997.

Sykes combined the achievements and appointments of several of his predecessors: the ecclesiastical authority of bishop was shared with 'R.R.' Williams (Bishop of Leicester), a previous university professorship with Dawson Dawson-Walker, and, like Sidney Nowell Rostron, he was a graduate of St John's College, Cambridge.

As he said: 'I knew the college reasonably well, [but] it seemed to me important not to presume that I knew it better than I did … My personal perception on arrival in college in September 1999 was of a confident and purposeful institution, into which it was a pleasure to be welcomed. At the end of my first year I am conscious that there are significant changes afoot … but the foundations of competence and effectiveness have been very well laid' (*College Record*, 2000).

The first year of Sykes' principalship saw some major staff changes. Dr Margaret Masson left after seven years as senior tutor, as did Dr Gillian Boughton, whose connection with St John's spans almost 30 years, both to take up posts at other Durham colleges (Margaret to St Chad's, Gill to St Mary's; both continued teaching in the English department). Other changes were made in the tutorial staff. James and Dawn Cook 'provided everyone with a remarkable example of a very public married life, and provided stability and kindness to many more students than were on their tutorial lists' (*College Record*, 2000); both were fully involved with the life of college, on the sports fields (particularly football) and at the Centre for Christian Communication. In

2005 Sykes led the farewells to two long-serving tutors, Helen Innes (13 years) and Ian Andrew (11 years).

The input of fresh blood into the tutorial team and Sykes's aim to employ the 'brightest and best' tutorial staff began immediately, as Dr Chloe Starr began work as senior tutor in 1999. She was succeeded by the Revd Dr Stephen Hampton in 2004 (he become a minor canon in 2005). It was Sykes's hope that the joy of working in the unique environment of St John's college would be reflected in the development of the employees in a 'humane and human institution'.

Chloe Starr (senior tutor 1999–2004) writes: 'A senior tutor remembers an odd mix of people and events. Catering surveys (the

Haughton dining room was developed as an 'exhibition space', a space for hanging commissioned pictures which altered regularly, rather than old group portraits. Perhaps appropriately enough, Stephen Sykes' portrait now hangs above the cutlery section, still making enquiries to students over the breakfast table!

final banishment of black bean sauce), communion services and bathtub raft races across the Wear. Interminable committee meetings over funding issues merge in the mind with long deliberations over occupancy rates and Information Technology at St Margaret's Garth. University drives for transferable skills programmes for undergraduates combine in memory with debates over the health and safety implications of bar towels at St John's bar committee. University threats to cut the independent colleges' central grant hovered over college for much of the early 2000s, forcing a mustering of financial and legal clout, and forging closer links with St Chad's. While planning and preparation went on behind closed doors for drastic financial scenarios, St John's reigned in university-wide student satisfaction surveys, students rating us top or second in successive years over a comprehensive range of indices from tutorial quality to bathroom appliances. Applications rates per place continued to increase as St John's reputation spread (a more professional website putting a new gloss on this process), and graduate student numbers reached a critical mass. What a senior tutor really remembers, however, are countless images of individuals. The student with a life-threatening illness who graduated successfully after zillions of requests for essay extensions; an emailed photo from a smiling student doing voluntary work abroad. A thank-you card, years later, from a student whose 2.2 degree was a huge achievement. Laughter and low-cut dresses in a freezing cold tent on Linton Lawn in November; bucking rodeos in Leech Hall and sumo wrestlers outside on St John's Day. Superb singing from our choir in the cathedral, and awful pantomimes, with mandatory college officer participation, at Christmas. (Fortunately the video camera only made its appearance at the end of my tenure, for Larry Snotter.) A succession of witty JCR Presidents whose speeches at official dinners mocked the more bizarre aspects of adolescent community life, as well as those who managed it. And last but not least, the parents, whose appearances at graduation suddenly made all things comprehensible. "Ah, Mrs Jones, so you're the mother of Petunia."[1]

Changes were also afoot in Cranmer Hall: a new director of the Wesley Study Centre in 2000, Dr Roger Walton; the establishment of Methodist Foundation training and the appointment in January 2005 of the first female warden of Cranmer Hall, Canon Dr Anne Dyer.

As every previous principal has found, work on the college buildings was a constant, embodying a continual struggle to give much care and attention to keep them in good condition and to adapt to the needs of the expanding college in the 21st century, including improvements to college roofs. To cope with college expansion Information Technology cabling was extended to allow internet access from student

A selection of staff celebrating the erection of a 'temporary' gazebo on Linton Lawn in Summer 2005.

rooms rather than just in the Cottage computer room. In 2000 42 student rooms were totally refurbished (*College Record*, 2000). At the end of a lengthy process the Tristram Room was revitalized by the loan of five pictures from the Founders' Collection in the Bowes Museum. 'This fine 18th-century room finally looks fully dressed, and completes a process begun many years ago by Principal Hickinbotham' (*College Record*, 2005).

In 2005 Sykes headed the 'energetic transformation of our fine gardens', particularly the garden between Leech Hall and Cruddas, and a summer gazebo was erected on Linton Lawn.

Olav

Alumni from the 1960s may remember a stuffed alligator appearing at the Principal's foot on formal college photographs. The story is that in 1961 a team of Johnian rowers found a real stuffed alligator on the riverbanks and proposed a motion in the Junior Common Room that it be adopted as the college mascot. That October, King Olav V of Norway visited the UK on a state visit, spending three days in the northeast. St John's alligator was paraded outside Palace Green in honour of this visit, and thus became known as 'Olav'.

A few years later, with his stuffing falling out, he was given a full Viking send-off, doused in paraffin, set alight and pushed to Valhalla down the Wear.

Until his 'resurrection' in 2005. JCR President, Roddy Peters noticed there was no Johnian mascot. Instead of the obvious eagle, a full-length costume was purchased with the support of the JCR, christened Olav II.

with thanks to Roddy Peters

The Borderlands Project

Chloe Starr (senior tutor 1999–2004) writes: 'Borderlands was Stephen Sykes's brainchild, an integrated academic, political and theological project from a college that was itself situated in between the academy and the Church. The journal *Borderlands* explored the range of this interdisciplinary territory, with articles on, among other topics, what constitutes Christian education, human rights laws and religious liberty, the relationship between theology and business, and the theology of alcohol.

'Borderlands encouraged the breaking down of constricting disciplinary barriers, and the positive engagement of Christian academics in wider reflection on their field. In an era of city academies and faith schools, serious academic thinking on the role of religion in education, and particularly in tertiary education, was timely. Borderlands bursaries were won by graduate students from both John's Hall and Cranmer to enable them to pursue topics from economics to film and art, all combining theological reflection with disciplinary inquiry. Talks in college by these bursary holders proved engaging, giving more time for discussion than the grand annual lectures.

'These [lectures] were, of course, the highlight of the Borderlands project, beginning, presciently, with Sir John Haughton on climate change. With the Vice-Chancellor introducing these lectures in one of the largest lecture halls the university afforded, the lectures showcased St John's intellectual vibrancy, presenting challenging issues to packed audiences of students and tutors. The dinners afterwards were much fun, too, with a memorable moment when Cherie Blair grimaced at Stephen Sykes for making her lead a further discussion on law and feminism in the middle of her duck à l'orange.'

The title Borderlands was taken from a book by D.M. Mackinnon (who taught Sykes at Cambridge), who used the word to indicate that theology could be done properly only if it constantly worked in the borders of the discipline.

The Borderlands lectures were:

- **2002:** Sir John Houghton CBE, FRS – 'Global Warming and Climate Change: A Scientific and Spiritual Challenge'
- **2003:** Professor Simon Conway Morris FRS – 'The Paradoxes of Evolution: Inevitable Humans in a Lonely Universe'
- **2004:** Cherie Booth QC – 'Justice: A Personal and Communal Challenge'
- **2005:** Archbishop Josiah Idowu-Fearon – 'Conflict and Cooperation Between Christians and Muslims in Nigeria'
- **2006:** Andrew Dilnot CBE – 'Christianity and Economics'
- **2007:** John Barrow FRS: 'Our Place in the Universe'
- **2008:** Dame Suzi Leather: 'Serving God & Caeser: Regulation & Faith'.

'Experience shows that the college is generally responsive to the care of its environment; it's just that universities tend not to make good gardeners' (*College Record*, 2005)

Commercial activities progressed well. 'Vacation Business [was] expanding significantly, under the expert direction of Paul Norris, commercial officer' (*College Record*, 2000), with conferences ranging from biblical studies to insectology.

Academic success also continued: 10 firsts were achieved in 2000, 18 in 2006, and a peak of 28 in 2005.

Rather than let the year end on a lull after the exams, Sykes worked with the JCR to provide a few cultural highlights in the post-exam summer weeks. Under the guidance of JCR President Roddy Peters, two open-air productions of Shakespeare were performed: *A Midsummer Night's Dream* in 2005 and *Much Ado About Nothing* the following year. These were 'magical' performances, put on in less than a week. It was an intense time for the players, but an experience enjoyed by all members. Following the storytelling tradition of 'tales around the fireside', Sykes also instigated a series of dramatized readings of *Beowulf* and *Sir Gawain and the Green Knight* in partnership with the English department.

Sykes re-instituted 6 May as the college feast, the feast day of St John Before the Latin Gate (*Ante portam latinum*). The date 6 May commemorates St John being thrown into a pot of boiling oil outside the Latin gate but emerging unscathed. (Thankfully, this isn't on the college crest, neither is it re-enacted in John's Day celebrations!)

Sykes retired in 2006. 'When I arrived in October 1999,' he has written, 'it seemed to me that I was joining a community with a confident and purposeful sense of its own identity. In lots of ways I believe I still have evidence that members of college continue to enjoy their experience of membership, and that the community as a whole makes an outstanding contribution to the life and reputation of the university. These have been, for me, personally, very good years indeed, in both halls. In Crammer I have had the pleasure of being part of a fine academic and formational enterprise; in John's Hall it has been immensely enjoyable to participate in numerous activities and to share my own enthusiasms. The diversity of college is one of its strengths; so too is its comparatively modest size. I leave it with a sense of profound gratitude, and with confidence in its future' (*College Record*, 2006).

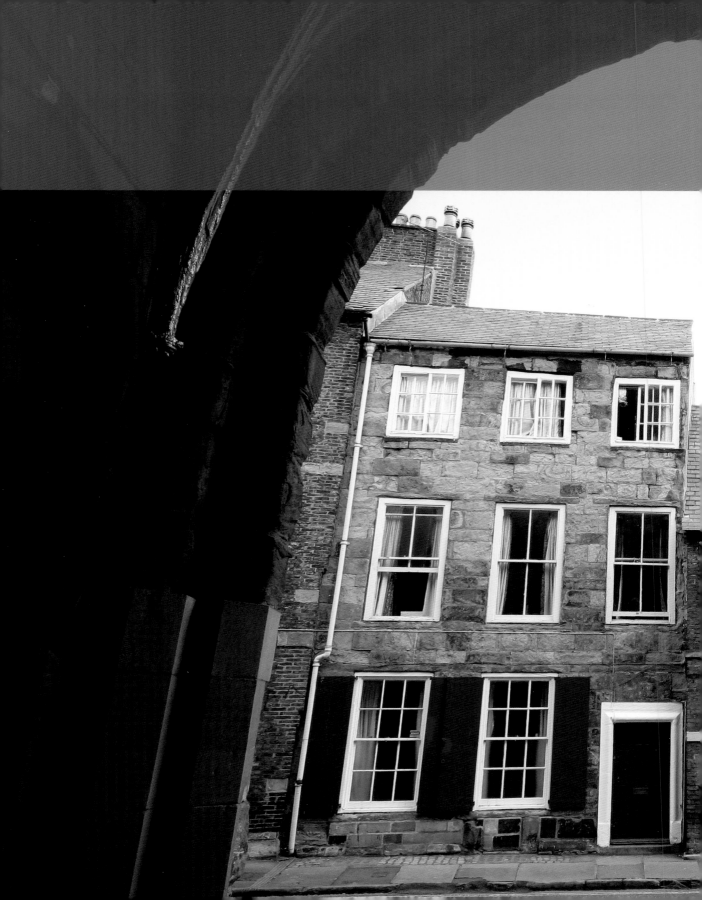

PART 2

Architecture and Administration

Cranmer Hall:
Celebrating the Jubilee 1958–2008

From humble beginnings with only five men in 1909, to around 50 men and women in recent years, some resident, others living with families, still more commuting and taking extension courses, in many respects, Cranmer Hall has changed with the times, but retains its evangelical, global and missionary focus. Students attend courses in preaching, pastoral work and mission in addition to academic lectures.

The catalyst for a separate training hall began under Principal Williams (1945–54). In 1951 Williams developed regular chapter meeting for 'the diploma group', distinct from the 'university group', with greater devotional expectations and separate dining arrangements. Under Principal Hickinbotham (1954–70) the college prepared itself both physically and organizationally for a formal separation. The new 'divinity hall' hoped that 'most St John's men will want to come to Cranmer Hall and will form the backbone of it and give it a distinctively Johnian character' (*Durham Johnian*, 1958) although graduates from other universities were encouraged. As numbers of 'Cranmerians' rapidly increased a new block was built including lecture rooms and study bedrooms, increasing the college's capacity to 120.

Cranmer Hall formally opened in 1958 as 'a separate theological college in association with St John's College, Durham … Cranmer Hall has its own self-contained gardens and buildings; its own teaching staff; and its own special way of life … [a] pattern of an ordered corporate life of study, prayer, and pastoral training' (Principal Hickinbotham, *Durham Johnian*,

1958 diploma group in lecture.

1958). The 1961 inspectors commented that 'the successful polarization of two distinct seminaries, under one control, attests to [Hickinbotham's] powers and singleness of heart … The hall is a home of sound theological learning in the best, that is to say the most charitable, evangelical tradition of the Church of England'. The hall's reputation attracted overseas students, including Benjamin Nwankiti (1957–60), later Bishop of Owerri, Nigeria, and John Watanabe, later Bishop of Hokkaido.

Staff Memories

Between 1968 and 1970 John Cockerton took on the responsibility of being the first 'warden' of Cranmer Hall with the oversight of around 40 ordinands. Most significantly, at this time, a certificate in theology was validated by the university in October 1978, taught in-house, and survived the storms of reduced funding for theological training.

The hall's second warden, Timothy Yates (1971–9), remembers: 'It was an immensely exciting and satisfying time. The [work] was intensive and highly concentrated, providing training for around 50 men and 25 women in training for ministry. The resource provided by the Durham faculty with luminaries like C.K. Barrett, C.E.B. Cranfield, H.E.W. Turner, S.W. Sykes and others was very valuable. We also had increasingly good relationships with Ushaw College after Vatican II. Between 1975 and 1979 a new Cranmer staff emerged, and I was greatly helped by Rosemary Nixon (the third woman tutor), Willie Morrice (a Church of Scotland minister, New Testament scholar and meticulous college librarian) amongst others.'

The appointment of Ian Bunting as first director of pastoral studies (1971–8) marked the beginning of significant developments in pastoral training: 'I was interested because my experience of theological training in the United States, particularly in pastoral training and fieldwork, had convinced me of the need for changes from the "clerical hints-and-tips" approach that had become common in England. Looking back on my 16 years of association with St John's College, my abiding memory is of an intentional learning community that could be frustrating and yet generously affirming of all kinds of insight and initiative that reflected the college motto. I think immediately of Traidcraft, the students from overseas, college missions, a visit to the coalface in Langley Moor, social action on the Gilesgate estate, and St John's undergraduate Pastoralia teams leading Sunday worship in depressed ex-mining villages.'

During the 1970s the extensions studies programme increased in scope and diversity. Michael Williams, director of pastoral studies from 1978, recalls: 'The Urban Studies Unit in Gateshead became an integral part of the course offered in Cranmer Hall,

The Library Lawn.

reflecting a concern that ordinands should have the experience of the inner city; the first in the north of England. The first director was Carl Kuusk, one of our own former students.'

Christopher Byworth (warden 1979–83) reflects: 'Of over 40 years of ordained ministry, the brief four years at Cranmer were probably my most formative. I enjoyed the studying and teaching almost as much as the pastoral contacts of some 65 to 80 ordinands a year. This period was an era of change within the Church of England: liturgically, in the pattern of ministry and training, and charismatic renewal. Women priests were an issue for a few. We had never fewer than 25 women ordinands in any one year. This was, by some margin, the largest number in any UK theological college, and we had a woman principal [Ruth Etchells 1979–88] and at least one other woman staff member. It has been a huge privilege to have been warden of Cranmer. I received outstanding love and I met and married my beloved wife, Ruth. What more could I ask for? Thanks be to God.'

Ian Cundy (warden 1983–92), one of the bishop's inspectors for Cranmer's 1982 inspection, had the unusual task of implementing some of his own recommendations. He found the college 'very welcoming and friendly, crammed into a series of complex and unsuitable buildings, well adapted for their use, housing a community with a real sense of identity.' The major

John Cockerton

John Cockerton, first warden of Cranmer Hall (1968–70) and principal (1970–8) remembers: 'In my time, the college stood for an inclusive evangelicalism, with high academic standards in a warm and friendly community as at least I found it to be: worship, study, evangelism, fellowship combined to make it a wonderfully satisfying place to work and I believe a good training environment with deep relationships among the staff which have long outlasted our time serving together.'

The first year diploma group, 1954: back row: Ian Knox, John Oliver, Joe Hall, John Southgate, Leslie Stanbridge, Don Philpot. front: Bill Matthews, Stuart Brindley, Ian Smith, Richard McDermid, Alan Voke.

development at this time was the 1991 validation of the Cranmer degree in theology and ministry.

The Wesley Study Centre was opened in 1988. Roger Walton, director since 1999 reflects: 'Back in 1988 the Methodist Church set up a small-scale training unit in Durham to work with Cranmer Hall and Ushaw College, with six part-time students and a part-time director. The WSC has prospered, growing from that small beginning to an average of 30 students a year over the last ten years, most of them full-time, and many people in the northeast

have discovered and acted on God's call to ministry in a variety of ways. In 2007 the WSC was designated one of only three centres in the UK for full-time training for Methodist ministers and the lead training institution for Yorkshire and the northeast.

St John's College has provided the ideal environment for the WSC to grow and develop. The warm hospitality experienced made us feel at home and valued, and the open evangelical ethos has struck a resonant chord for most Methodist students and staff. In 2002 the Methodist Church signed a memorandum of association with St John's College to recognize and strengthen our shared life.'

John Pritchard (warden 1993–6) remembers that: 'It was in my time as Warden that we were hit substantially with the fore waves of the row over human sexuality that has engulfed the Anglican communion since [primarily over a particular placement parish]. At the same time Michael Vasey, our illustrious liturgy tutor and Cranmer institution, chose to publish his long-awaited book on homosexuality, *Strangers and Friends*. The balloon went up again!'

Courses were further integrated with the university, a dedicated MA appeared on the horizon, new teaching facilities were developed. The Urban Studies Unit was transformed into the Urban Mission Centre [under director Pete Wilcox, later Steven Burns].

Stephen Croft (warden 1996–2004) also has a long association with St John's, having read Classics at St John's in the mid-1970s, and returned as ordinand 1980–3, becoming president of Cranmer Common Room. He remembers his years

Cranmer Hall in 1966. The following October, the first female students were to be admitted.

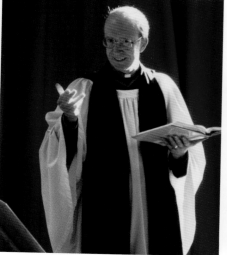

Below: Joy and Stephen Sykes with Ian Cundy, former warden of Cranmer Hall and President of College Council, outside St Mary-the-Less at Principal Sykes' farewell service in 2006.

Above: Cranmer Hall tutors at Grease themed staff lunch c.2005: Gavin Wakefield, David Clough, Roger Walton, Steve Croft (warden), Alan Bartlett.

Right: John Pritchard (warden 1993–6) remembers that at St John's, 'nothing stood still for long. If it did it would get painted by Bill and Ted. And through it all, many ordinands, and the increasing number of independent students, were expertly taught. The Church of England was enriched with some excellent clergy. It was a good time.'

as warden as: 'Primarily lots of good people, both students and staff. Working hard to show prospective students round and encourage them to Durham. Lots of joy. Lots of learning (for me). Lots of hard work. Being stretched in the teaching. Trying to build a strong team. Weighing decisions about people very carefully. Making mistakes and getting some things right.

'The middle years of my time as warden were marked by a number of untimely deaths, including Michael Vasey and a number of current or recently ordained students and their families. Grieving together marked the community. The mix of minor and major keys in the psalms came alive in new ways. And the best bits? Slowly growing working relationships with colleagues in the support staff, John's and Cranmer. Cake at tutors' meetings. Courtesy and conversation. Watching people learn and grow as they worship and live and study together. Having time to write in the midst of it all. College missions. St John's is and remains a place of love and hope and faith. Long may it remain so.'

In the 1990s Cranmer had the third highest number of ordinands of any college in the country. In 1996 numbers reached over 100, the largest number of any theological college in the country. Cranmer also had a good academic reputation, with the Cranmer-based degree in theology and ministry, revalidated for a further five years. In 2001 an MA in theology and ministry was developed, alongside a diploma in ministry.

Overseas students have always been attracted to studying at Cranmer Hall. In 2001 Cranmer hosted five students from Africa, one each from Fiji, Romania and Australia. The first Alphonse Mohapi Scholar, Mr Atwell Xana, part of Durham Diocesan Link with Lesotho. arrived in 2001.

Anne Dyer, warden since 2005 looks to the future thus: 'The challenges of the most recent years have been balanced by the excitement of being part of an Anglican theological establishment, which attracts high-quality ordinands with a passion for God's mission understood in wide and generous ways. Partnerships [between dioceses, churches and wider communities] have built on existing longstanding relationships; it really is part of Cranmer Hall's DNA to be working with and learning from others.

'So, these early years of the 21st century are marked by this season of looking out and responding to God's call to engage in mission in the world, seen most clearly in the community's response to having a Sudanese bishop studying at Cranmer in 2005. The Rt Revd Francis Loyo, Bishop of the Diocese of Rokon, located in no-man's-land during the Sudanese Civil War, had an immense impact on Cranmer. Living humbly among us and speaking often of his peoples' suffering, Bishop Francis was a much-loved member of Cranmer Hall. Out of love for him, and to support the people of Rokon as they struggled to recover once peace was declared, the Edith Jackson Trust was established. The trust is supporting a project to build a school for Rokon, and this aim has encouraged generous giving of time and resources by the students of Cranmer Hall and the Wesley Study Centre.

'Cranmer stands for a hospitable and generous orthodoxy and will be looking to be part of the public face of open evangelicalism for years to come.'

My most abiding memories of St John's are immensely happy and fulfilling; lifelong friendships and preparation for service.

David Grieve, John's Hall, 1970–4

Buildings and Estates

A large part of how one remembers St John's College is the distinctive nature of the Bailey buildings, a constant challenge to upkeep and navigate. Most of the college buildings were originally occupied by members of the garrison and court of the prince bishops, and they have fascinating histories, dating back to the 15th century. The college now consists of a continuous and fully connecting line of attractive Georgian buildings. Former occupants of Number 4, Bowes House, include Katherine, the widow of Dean Whittingham (the translator of the Geneva Bible) and half-sister of reformer Jean Calvin, and the Bowes-Lyon and Eden families. A regular visitor was Alice Liddell, a friend of the Bowes family and the inspiration for Lewis Carroll's *Alice in Wonderland*. Margaret Masson remembers: 'The quirkiness of the building, the result of many reshapings, was a joy: remember the stairs leading up somewhere above the bar that abruptly stopped? The secret and multiple ways to get from a to b?'

Writing in 1913, Principal Dawson-Walker had noted: 'The accommodation [in Number 6] was soon found to be inadequate. Number 19 North Bailey was then secured [now St Chad's]. Soon afterwards Number 4 South Bailey was purchased from Prebendary Fox, and the purchase of the High School from the university (Number 3) is in process of being completed.' As early as 1919, Charles Wallis wrote in the *Old Johnian* that: 'Practically all my energy has been spent this last half year on the work of "reconstruction". The college was in a shocking state of dilapidation.'

David Day summarized the challenge faced by successive principals for the upkeep of college: 'Our ancient buildings are a joy and an undiluted delight but there are bound to be local difficulties when 200 young people live in a series of stately homes' (*College Record*, 1995). In 1998 he remarked: 'Sometimes the place resembles a building site, sometimes a menagerie, occasionally a four-star hotel and less frequently the Athenaeum.'

Number 6 South Bailey, currently the entrance to Cranmer Hall, was the first property occupied by St John's Hall in 1909, purchased along with Number 4 (Bowes House) and Number 3 (Haughton) in 1912. Tom Thompson (1956–60) remembers: 'John Hughes and I shared a room on the top floor of 6 South Bailey during 1956–7. There was a fire escape harness in our room. John tried it out and became stuck in it just outside the window, but too low to climb back inside the room, causing quite a crowd to gather outside! I think the harness was a wartime contraption,

Above: The Quad in the 1970s, around which the William Leech Hall was built in 1987.

Right: Heraldic plaque on the side of number 4 South Bailey, formerly belonging to the Bowes family.

Number 23 North Bailey, the farthest north of St John's with distinctive Johnian blue paintwork.

The Bailey Buildings: a reflection

'I discovered that the entrance to Cranmer Crossroads marks the line of a medieval vennel, that the gap in the wall by Cruddas was part of a shrewdly negotiated deal by the cathedral cellarer, John Rodes, that the widow of Dean Whittingham who translated the Geneva Bible, lived in Number. 4, that Sir Robert Eden brought his young bride, aged 19, to live in Number 3 in 1739 and that they had 11 children. This is the stuff of soap opera, and it has bred in me a fresh appreciation of the buildings in which we work. Nor is it just a matter of buildings. I was moved to read of Henry Watson Fox who worked as a missionary in India, lost his wife, child and father before coming back to the Bailey to die, aged 31, full of faith and confidence in Christ … Institutions need to value the best of their past but if they live in a welter of antiquarian nostalgia and sentimentalism, they perish.'

David Day, *College Record*, 1995

made from webbing – of course the war had only ended about ten years previously. He was in that position for quite some time, but I can't remember how we got him down, but we did, none the worse, except that his pride had suffered!'

For about 60 years the principal lived in a self-contained flat in Bowes House, in what is now the Senior Common Room. Principal Wallis even held musical evenings in his living room. Cecily Williams, in her 1961 memoir, remembers: 'I loved our flat … [above the college office and Senior Common Room]. Charlie [Wallis], who had retired to a residence opposite the college, urged me to see that only the quietest students were given rooms above us. Having slept through a considerable part of each Blitz I could not believe that the most riotous students would disturb us … Our flat was in a Queen Anne building, and we had the most lovely panelled dining room with a wrought-iron fireplace and subdued wall-lights … We were on the college central heating system, and there were shutters to all our windows. The bleak

northern winters were some of the cosiest we have ever spent.' When John Cockerton married Diana Smith in 1974, the flat was converted into a smaller set of rooms; Rosemary Nixon, women's and Old Testament tutor and first non-principal resident from 1975, remembers it as 'a comfortable haven.'

The Senior Common Room is now on the first floor of Bowes House, significantly renovated in 1997. It is 'graceful, quiet and spacious, heightened by period detail and delightful discoveries, the best of which are probably the three intact perfect examples of 18th-century and very early 19th-century fireplaces which were discovered complete behind institutional hardboard' (Gillian Boughton, *College Record,* 1998). 'Quirks' remain and the original door locks on the guest room are 'wonderful' (Howard Stevens).

The entrance to Number 3 South Bailey, formerly Durham High School for Girls, purchased by St John's Hall in 1912 and renamed after the Cruddas family's ancestral home, Haughton Castle.

Below: Jude *filming on Bailey: Georgina Wilczek (nee Luck) remembers, 'In the October of 1996, the John's section of the Bailey was turned into a filmset for a production of* Jude the Obscure *[starring Christopher Eccleston and Kate Winslet]. They poured lots of ash and rubble onto the road to cover up the double yellow lines. The shot ended up being a brief shot of someone running across the Bailey from the cathedral archway and banging on the door of 28 North Bailey.'*

Opposite:
The South
Bailey buildings.

NUMBER 3 SOUTH BAILEY, HAUGHTON HOUSE

St John's main reception building, Number 3 South Bailey, was bought in 1912 and is named after the Cruddas family's Northumberland home. It drew together college's two 'halves', Numbers 6 and 4 South Bailey, along with Number 19 North Bailey. The house, with its remarkable Georgian stone façade (significantly restored in 1996), was originally rented from the university, before which it was Durham High School for Girls. The lease for Number 3 included 'the Cottage' (known as Number $3\frac{1}{2}$), which was used as additional student accommodation from October 1912. It is now used as a computer room and chaplain's office.

Neil Robinson (ordinand in 1950s) remembers: 'The building at the heart of St John's was Haughton, a large, imposing house fronting on to South Bailey. In that cluster of buildings were housed student rooms, the principal's home, the dining room and kitchen, the Junior and Senior Common Rooms and the library.' George Parkinson (1944–8) remembers that the post was placed on a huge table in the entrance hall, then the JCR, each morning.

In the 1970s Haughton House developed as an 'administrative centre'. Under Principal Day the space was opened up to provide an expansive and impressive welcome to visitors and students alike. The Eden staircase was restored, and the reception office was opened up with glass doors. Noticeboards and display cabinets were put up, and pictures of the principals lined the staircase. A glass panel was put directly opposite the entrance, blocking off the corridor to the dining room.

Chris Edmonson (1968–73) remembers: 'When John Cockerton became principal he addressed students from both John's and Cranmer, outlining his vision for the next few years, at the heart of which was his hope that there would be no division between the two, but that we might be "one great whole". The dining room erupted with laughter, with a different understanding of whole/hole, not least because of the then quite dilapidated state of the buildings!'

Right: Cranmer Hall in the 1970s.

Left: Sue Hobson and Gill Stewart on the Eden staircase.

NUMBERS 1 AND 2 SOUTH BAILEY, LINTON HOUSE

Linton House, named after the first Anglican bishop alumnus from St John's, was exchanged with St Chad's college in 1963, along with Number 28 North Bailey and Number 1 South Bailey (swapped for Numbers 22 and 22a North Bailey). Linton Wing was also included. This was a mixed blessing because the rooms were in a variable state of repair and (are still) very small. Linton House was refurbished and restructured in 1994. 'The effect has been startling. What was hardly the best face of St John's has been transformed. If you come to Durham you should ask for a guided tour' (David Day, *College Record,* 1995).

NUMBER 23 NORTH BAILEY

This remains a separate college 'house', divided by St Chad's accommodation between. It houses 16 students on four floors, a tutor's room, laundry and kitchen. It was refurbished and used as an outdoor activities centre in 1997 under the leadership of Rob Bianchi, a former JCR President. Georgina Wilczek (née Luck) remembers: 'Chris Lyth, Mark Tindale and Lucas Sneller once

abseiled down the back of 23 North Bailey. Chris was a great climber and even managed to scale across to my room on the outside of Brockwell F (second floor) [St Margaret's Garth] to sneakily remove my keyboard as part of a practical joke.'

NUMBER 7 SOUTH BAILEY, PRINCIPAL'S ACCOMMODATION

Among the college staff who have lived in Number 7 are John and Diana Cockerton in 1975, Ruth Etchells and Ian and Jo Cundy. (Michael and Joan Ramsey lived opposite throughout the 1980s.) Since 1997 Number 7 has become a fully functioning crèche for Cranmer and the wider community. It also houses the postgraduate centre, which is notoriously difficult to find. The postgraduate rooms consist of a small computer room and a common room, which are much valued!

THE LIBRARY

Following the 1974–7 development campaign, the 'new chapel', originally intended for sole undergraduate use, became the college library; both halls united their worship into one chapel in 1975. The library was extended, funded by the Esmee Fairbairn Foundation, and a gallery, designed by Professor Murta of Sheffield, was added to give additional space for non-theological texts and study carrels. The gallery was intended to 'provide for

The home of Cranmer Creche, number 7 South Bailey.

our needs for the next 20 or 30 years' so is possibly due for renewal in the near future.

The library had 11,000 volumes in 1977. It currently has about 30,000 books, three-quarters of which are theology. It is the main resource for Cranmer students and a good one for theology students. Because students had begun to bring in their own lamps, in the summer of 2005 new lighting was installed, and the library is now four times brighter. The desk lights were removed, but the old desks remain.

College in the 1970s

Rosemary Nixon remembers: 'I soon discovered John's was even more of a rabbit warren than Cranmer. The place creaked, floor levels were uncertain and student beds were supported by bricks or books. The whole place was dilapidated. But the cellar was being dug out for a bar!'

The electronic Auto-Lib system was installed in 1999. 'Zapping a book with a hand-held, *Star Wars* stun gun firing red rays is much more exciting than filling in a boring old borrowing card. Some of us go down of an evening and borrow and return books which we have no intention of reading just for the pleasure of vaporising Klingons' (Principal Day, *College Record*, 1999).

GARDENS

The individual houses along the Bailey all had considerable gardens running down to the River Wear, and in 1921 the Durham University *Journal* described the gardens as containing 'one of the best preserved sections of the [medieval] wall', which was used as a store for ice from the Wear. In 1933–4 a quadrangle at the back of Number 7 was paved and became known as the Wallis Garden (it was relaid in 1975). The Principal's Walk down to the riverbank also developed. Cecily Williams remembers: 'The college gardens were glorious; shady lawns, paved court and

Stories from the Tool Shed

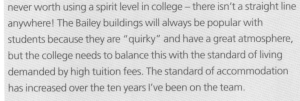

Alan Usher, head of maintenance since 1998, writes: 'I've come to realize that care for St John's College is 90 per cent reactive, only 10 per cent proactive. I work with a good team, all of whom came for short-tem jobs and have ended up staying! I am very proud of the college buildings, that they are not a National Trust show home, but a place for students to live and work. The damage and vandalism in college is very low compared to other colleges; sometimes things come off in students' hands, but that's because they are old, not broken on purpose! We've discovered it's never worth using a spirit level in college – there isn't a straight line anywhere! The Bailey buildings will always be popular with students because they are "quirky" and have a great atmosphere, but the college needs to balance this with the standard of living demanded by high tuition fees. The standard of accommodation has increased over the ten years I've been on the team.

'Very few people know that the college is gradually making its way towards the river. In a thousand years time they will be great riverside apartments! Georgian houses were built to move, but it's only at a rate of about 1 millimetre a year. Leech Hall has very solid foundations, so one day it might be overtaken by Bowes House! The old buildings are like an old granny: they need constant maintenance and can smell a lot! I've also buried a series of time capsules around college, but won't tell you where.'

Above: Inside the College Library.

Right: The College gardens c.1930s.

Below: The Library as seen from Cranmer Hall.

a wonderful terrace high above the River Wear … It seemed bliss indeed, and when I discovered a clump of autumn-flowering gentians on the rockery, my cup of happiness was full.'

CRUDDAS HOUSE

At the opening of Cruddas on 14 March 1913 Eleanor Cruddas declared: 'In the faith of Jesus Christ we declare these buildings opened. Within these walls may truth, faith, and the fear of God, together with Christian love and sound learning, for ever abound.'

The house was closed to students in the 1940s, housing RAF cadets instead and, later, displaced students from St Mary's. Johnians were again housed in Cruddas after demob. George Parkinson (1944–8) remembers living in Cruddas: 'Numbers of students had risen rapidly to about 70 by the start of that year, the war having finished and young men at liberty to return to academic pursuits. I liked living in that part of college as, compared to the rest, it was modern, with the luxury of central heating to keep out the cold.' John Hunter (1946–9) lived in Cruddas throughout this time: 'Excellent accommodation.'

Later students have been less enthusiastic. 'Student accommodation was basically primitive, but it had its advantages. Water fights [in Cruddas] were standard' (David Grieve 1970–4). 'Cruddas corridors were covered in linoleum, leading to frequent water fights, often with binfuls of water sloshing around the floor.

The windows above the doors are alleged to be used as spy holes for when women were entertained; in which case, the student's bed had to be removed into the corridor' (Jane Grieve, née Piérsénné, 1973–6). A more recent undergraduate describes Cruddas as 'an idiosyncratic building – entrance on the top floor, and descending down towards the river with rooms varying from the pokey to the palatial' (Richard Horton, 1983–6).

CRANMER HALL

Principal Hickinbotham oversaw the building of Cranmer Hall and the undergraduate chapel (later library), launched by the ten-year jubilee appeal. Teaching rooms were originally in Numbers 4–7 South Bailey, with the new block built between Numbers 5 and 6. 'The Barn', the annex to Number 6, and old stables on the quadrangle were demolished. The study accommodation increased to 45–50 Cranmer students, a college total of 120. Joy Wishlade (née Hickinbotham) remembers: 'The building site became our playground. Our enjoyment ranged from climbing on the scaffolding, biking through the mud created by the building and befriending the builders, having tea with one of the builders' families! Once we tipped a bag of lime down a drain to see what happened; of course, it set solid and neither the builders nor my parents were amused!'

By 1958, according to the Principal's Letter of that year, 'Cranmer Hall has its own self-contained gardens and buildings; its own teaching staff; and its own special way of life … and a new heating system has been installed. In Number 4 there is the library, the Common Room (formerly the SCR) and the dining hall of the old reading room.'

Room (without) a View

In 1971, Warden Timothy Yates received the following letter: 'When the Psalmist wrote about "going down to the pit" he must have had in mind Cruddas 44, that enchanting cream and blue sentry box at the darkest end of the well. Although small, the room does have some features which are not generally shared throughout the college: no sunlight hours, a panoramic view of an ancient wall tastefully decorated with various species of moss and assorted fungi, and a row of dustbins which are notoriously famous during the warmer months for smells which would make the Italian Tourist Board green with envy. Regardless of seasons, and at all times of the day and night, there is the WC 1 piece orchestra playing 4/4 time behind the thin partition wall; I believe it has been resident since the building was erected. Our benefactor must have been greatly appreciative of the arts. Finally, there is the greatest novelty of all, made possible by a piece of fiendish architectural genius: the bath outlet pipe. This pipe, thanks to early 20th-century building skills, actually comes through into the room and runs underneath the bed before vanishing through the outside wall, thus giving the effect of a private built-in Niagara Falls. This particular novelty is best appreciated during the early hours of the morning as it chugs and splurges beneath the bedsprings in its desperate haste to reach the

sea. For all its shortcomings, strangely enough I have become quite attached to my little pad – after all it is quite novel. However, sentiment must be put aside and a hopeful request submitted: PLEASE CAN I HAVE ANOTHER ROOM NEXT YEAR? Yours, very sincerely, Bill Worley [Cranmer Hall 1969–72].'

(In recent years this particular room has been given a function more in keeping with its personality: a toilet and shower room! – Ed. note)

Left: College grounds of Number 6 showing 'the barn' and stables demolished for the new undergraduate chapel, now the College library.

Above: William Leech (far right) after the 1987 opening. Ruth Etchells is displaying the Queen Mother's portrait presented after her formal opening of the new hall.

building materials to the site. I regard it as little short of miraculous that the planners allowed the builders to take down the Bailey wall of Cranmer dining hall, and run a small railway from the Bailey to the site through Cranmer dining hall. It had

WILLIAM LEECH HALL

Apart from Cruddas House, the William Leech Hall is the most significant building project on the Bailey site. Principal Etchells remembers in the late 1970s: 'There was a strong sense of the inadequacy of our buildings socially, and the need for a "multi-purpose hall", plans for which figured in council discussions from the mid-1970s.' Leech Hall opens onto Cruddas and a small garden area. It was designed by Tony Hyland of Hayton, Lee & Braddock and built by G. W. Lazenby. The hall is named after William Leech, the benefactor of a northeast charity.

Rosemary Nixon remembers: 'When the bulldozer, concrete mixer and building equipment had to be brought to the site through Cranmer dining room, we knew there was no going back!' Etchells remembers that a major difficulty 'was access for

Above: Number 6 South Bailey.

Right: Any Questions, hosted by Jonathan Dimbleby, was broadcast live from the Leech Hall in St John's College on 14 March 2008. Panel members included Danny Alexander MP, Lord Geoffrey Howe, Baroness Haleh Afshar OBE and Nick Brown MP. The hall was filled to capacity with 206 guests.

been a complex construction task, with many tonnes of earth having to be removed by a dumper truck through Cranmer dining room – a wide space having been temporarily made across two window openings. You can see the signs in the mortar to this day, from the reconstruction of the windows as the project was completed. These excavations lowered the roofline of the new hall of sufficient size for its intended purposes. The other difficulty it is now hard to imagine is with what hostility the process of its building was greeted by members of the Junior Common Room.'

Etchells realized the significant disruption that would be caused and gathered the student body into Haughton dining room (the only space large enough for gatherings): 'We are going to build a hall. It will be a nightmare. Some of you won't like it.' Protests were held, and some building work was disturbed, but once the hall was opened 'the pride of the student body in their hall was immediate and immense. Later generations cannot conceive how life could have been lived without it. Leech Hall has been a brilliant asset to the college, and the day the Queen Elizabeth, the Queen Mother, came to open it was a highlight for

This Hall built through the munificence of WILLIAM LEECH was opened on 25th June 1987 by HER MAJESTY QUEEN ELIZABETH THE QUEEN MOTHER

the college in the 1980s. There is no doubt whatever that Leech Hall has met many, many needs, not least as a "cross-over point" between John's and Cranmer, where shared activities can take place. But it has also proved itself as an immense asset in attracting vacation trade; it is a favourite venue for university lectures and concerts and drama, and it is the natural place not only to hold college parties but to meet for worship that is shared by the two halls (particularly Tuesday evening Eucharist).'

Peter Forster (senior tutor 1983–91), certainly appreciated the importance of Leech Hall for artistic events: 'The arrival of Leech Hall opened up opportunities for collaboration across the college. Plays were staged, and a range of social activities was held, including the ubiquitous discos. Public lectures attracted hundreds, including one by Stephen Sykes, before he became principal, on the Future of Anglicanism. Above all, Leech Hall permitted a weekly college Eucharist which all could attend, without the severe constraints of space in the college chapel.'

CELLAR BAR

Geoffrey Nutting (1955–8) remembers: 'The college I knew as an undergraduate was in every way a more sedate and sober institution than the one that, in 2006, I caught up with as its "visiting fellow". The least of this was alcoholic. Prohibition was anyway honoured more in the breach than in the strict observance. But I remember one occasion when a handful of us undergraduates, proposing a party with real drinks, felt special precaution was called for. With his permission, we held it in the safety of the college room of a nominal staff member.'

The cellar bar, 2008.

In the early 1970s there were lengthy debates in the college council about the morality of housing an alcoholic bar in a Christian evangelical training college. The decision was eventually made to develop the bar because it would be safer for students to buy and consume alcohol on college premises rather than in local pubs, although, of course, students are encouraged to mix with other colleges and go into town. The profits would be kept in-house because the bar was to be run by the JCR, providing extra income and work experience for Johnians. Former senior tutor Peter Forster corrects a few myths: 'For many years it had been believed that the founding documents of the college forbade a bar, but this eventually proved to be entirely false … The bar committee functioned best with a couple of keen undergraduates prepared to shoulder the main operational task, with a Cranmer student, perhaps with a financial background, maintaining the accounts. In my time I can recall Rob McClaren and Justin Welby as very effective bar accountants.'

In the summer of 1976 the first levels of cellars were dug out. Ken Kitchin, bursar, writing in 1981, noted; 'Many earlier generations of Johnians would not have countenanced such a place on these premises, and there was considerable debate about its building; but now it is a feature of the college. Situated in the cellars under Linton House it comprises two rooms linked by a low passage. The timbered ceilings, the restored fireplace, the wooden benches, the veteran pump and the excellent ales make it a very pleasant place in which to sit and relax. This feature helps to build up the community of the college. This is something John's has always valued, and we endeavour to continue.'

It is inevitable that the bar has not remained without controversy. Margaret Masson remembers: '"Bargate" was one of the low points during my term as senior tutor. Irregularities in the way the bar was being run were uncovered, which led to the bar being closed while this was investigated. In retrospect, the major issue was a culture of sloppiness and lack of rigour rather than large-scale dishonesty, but at the time it felt like a real betrayal of trust. On the other hand, the way so many students, realizing their part in this, came forward to own up, and the college meeting we had to clear the air was something very

Principal Cockerton in the cellar bar, 1970s.

officers with this wild idea. Financing the plan was an on–off–on-off comedy until the oranges and lemons finally stopped moving and we were in business. It was a superb venture of faith.'

John Hirst negotiated with the county council and secured the land with the old ward block. He remembers naming discussions: 'The college officers wanted to name the development in a meaningful way and felt that by using names of the coal seams surrounding it, Durham's mining heritage would not be forgotten. However, we didn't fully realize how odd these names were: Busty, Marshall, Maudlin, Hutton, Harvey, Gannister Clag, Bottom Brass Thill, Top Brass Thill and so on. We named the family enclave "Brass Thill". The explanation I was given is that a "thill" was the exposed face of the seam, which, because of the way the iron pyrites in it glinted in the beam of the miners' lamps, acquired the name "brass thill".'

David Day remembers: 'St Margaret's was the site of the old workhouse, a desperate place and much feared. Ruth Etchells gave me a copy of census returns for the place. They were heart-rending. So many women with children – clearly, sent to the workhouse when the breadwinner died. [As a way of remembering them,] at the opening ceremony I read aloud the names of about four families consisting of mother and children so that they might have a voice at last. It was another attempt (like the coal seams) to link the place with the people and city of Durham.'

special – Michael Vasey, the college liturgy tutor, saw it as a spontaneous rite of reconciliation and was thrilled to watch this in action! All of us learned a great deal from that episode!'

The bar is a regular focus for college social events. Phil Thomas (2003–6) remembers: 'Regular visits to the college bars gave opportunities to compare with John's, and you soon realized, yes, John's bar was tiny and yes, other colleges had a bigger range of drinks/big screens/other distractions, but our bar has a unique character, something I've appreciated more since I left. I'm yet to find anywhere like John's. Some of my best memories (and the best part of my budget) of my time at Durham were nights in the bar. Both my first and last nights as a student were spent there, and it's one of the main aspects of university life that's left its strongest mark. In the bar events committee (BEC) we organized themed events with assorted games, decorations and anything else we could within our £50 budget. Our three events, Tarts and Vicars, Roald Dahl and Saints and Sinners, saw members of college and staff make a fine effort to dress as Fantastic Mr Fox, Mr Twit, Oompa Loompas or plumb the depths of their creativity in dressing as a St Bernard or Sin Bin.'

St Margaret's Garth

The third significant development in college buildings was St Margaret's Garth, consisting of 25 student flats in five blocks, the Crossgate Centre and 12 family houses in Brass Thill. There was a long gestation period as college officers and council considered venues for new, affordable student accommodation throughout the late 1980s. However, as John Pritchard (warden 1993–6) remembers: 'It didn't pay to let John Hirst [bursar] off the lead for too long. He happened to be walking through the old St Margaret's Hospital site one day, saw it would soon be for sale and came back to the college

Top: John Gladwin opening St Margaret's Garth.

Right: The Cross Gate Centre.

Above: St Margaret's Garth (Victoria House) at the Garth's opening in October 1994 with unique Johnian bunting of college scarves.

Right: The Garth today, with the foundation stone laid by Stephen Sykes visible bottom left.

Senior tutor Margaret Masson remembers the opening with 'college scarves bedecking each window like bunting … and the staff going round praying in each and every flat before the start of the academic year. I remember the quizzically raised eyebrows when one particularly imaginative tutor committed to the Lord all the children that would be conceived there!'

David Day remembers the first residents moving in in the autumn of 1994; Cranmer families moved in in September 1994: 'On 1 October, a day that will live in my memory, a group of staff went down to welcome the John's Hall students. For eight and a half frenetic hours we took each individual student to his or her room and explained the mysteries of the electricity meter and the storage radiators. When I left at 7 pm, the place was a blaze of lights; potted plants and teddy bears had begun to appear on windowsills, the sound of the hi-fi was heard in the land; and a group of five students were just leaving one block and moving with purpose towards another.

'The senior tutor [Margaret Masson] and I have visited every flat, bearing gifts and making courteous inquiry about quality of life. We have been greatly encouraged by the almost universal delight of the residents and intrigued by the infinite variety of internal decoration and domestic routine. Already the folk myths are beginning to circulate. In an attempt to economize on electricity, so the tale is told, students in one house crawl along the carpet to avoid breaking the sensor beam that switches on the light … I am inordinately proud of the buildings … a year that

will turn bricks and breeze blocks into a living community. "Living at Margaret's" is already a stock phrase in college, though, as the freshers' handbook points out, it does not mean you are cohabiting with the senior tutor' (*College Record*, 1998).

In March 2007 a college estates strategy group was set up by the college council to survey the current buildings and to devise a strategy for the way forward. What emerged was, according to Principal David Wilkinson in March 2008, an 'unparalleled opportunity to form the college estate for the future, in a bold extension of resources on the Bailey'. Despite a significant capital works back-log on the Bailey properties, the renewed vision is to focus on the Bailey, to encourage a sense of community there in fit for purpose buildings that would allow the College to be a modern College on its historic site.

Potential future work could include selling the Crossgate Centre and St Margaret's flats (although not Brass Thill); new builds of an en-suited accommodation block on the library site; a new college study and learning centre; an extension of Haughton dining room to increase capacity and to deliver meals inside the dining room rather than across a main corridor; and an all-weather sports surface.

The college buildings and estates continue to provide challenges, but the college is proud to be able to offer hospitality for a wide range of conferences and events, including business meetings, day and residential conferences, retreats, summer schools and weddings.

What does Fides Nostra Victoria mean to me? Something like 'Faint heart never won anything'.
David Day, Principal 1992–9

St Mary-the-Less:
The Heart of St John's

Interior of St Mary-the-Less prior to the installation of the new east window in 1930.

It could be said that the heart of St John's College is the small chapel of St Mary-the-Less, which is on the west side of the Bailey. The chancel and nave are under separate roofs, with a bell turret containing two bells over the west gable (refurbished in 2005). The chapel has a total internal length of 64 feet 6 inches. It has been used as St John's College chapel since 1909. In 1919, when the parish became a united benefice with St Mary-le-Bow, the chapel was given to the college for 50 years. In 1927 it was given in perpetuity.

In a speech in 1930 Principal Nowell Rostron remembered: 'Wonderful quiet services in the tiny old church which we were allowed to use as our chapel, with the dim light of the oil lamps shining upon us, and the peace of that ancient house of God bathing our souls. In after years it has been altered and shaped for college needs, as we had no power to change it in those first days. Yet even then for some of us it was a place of spiritual vision and inspiration, for which we shall never cease to thank God.'

St Mary-the-Less was founded around 1140 by one of the Bulmers, Lords of Brancepeth, commemorated by the letter B in the stained glass windows, patronage passing to the Nevilles of Raby and then to the Crown. It is likely to have originally been used as a place of worship for the retainers and soldiers defending the city walls, although the total area of the parish was only 4 acres. The first rector known by name was Richard, who was appointed in 1300. He was followed in 1354 by Adam de Tanfield. In 1801 only 154 people lived in the North and South Bailey. In 1918 the parishes of St Mary-le-Bow and St Mary-the-Less were united, with the larger as the parish church. A strong connection remained, personified by Charles Wallis, who was rector of St Mary-le-Bow (1930–49)

The Cruddas Window

According to the 1930 *Old Johnian*, the former window 'was a very bad specimen of early Victorian art' and let in very little light. The window was designed by Christopher Webb of St Albans and was dedicated by Bishop Henson of Durham in October 1930, following the 1930 'coming of age'.

'The window has been designed on a plain quarry background in order to admit the maximum of light, contains the Crucifixion with the Blessed Virgin and St John (thus combining the dedications of the chapel and the college) grouped on a base which is Renaissance in character. A red curtain with orphrey of black and gold, suspended from the cross, throws into relief the figure of Our Lord. In the centre of the base is a shield containing the traditional Sacred Monogram on a red ground. Two angels above the main group hold a scroll containing the college motto "Fides Nostra Victoria", and at the foot there is an inscription commemorating benefactors: "To the glory of God. This window was erected in 1930 by members of St John's College in grateful memory of Dora Cruddas and all other benefactors of the college". Donations from Old Johnians amounted to £163 10s (now worth almost £5,500). (*Durham Johnian*, 1930)

in addition to being principal of St John's. Dennison, his butler, was St Mary-le-Bow's churchwarden.

The church, which was almost entirely rebuilt under Rector James Raine (1829–57), reopened on 16 November 1847. Its previous condition is described as 'a very mean looking edifice with low ceilings, sash windows and blue tiles'. Chevron mouldings were added to the plain Norman chancel arch, copies from the castle's gallery. The main doorway, which at first sight appears to be Norman, dates back to this restoration. Part of the stained glass in the south wall of the chancel contains fragments of old cathedral glass.

In the west wall is a monument to the Polish Count Borowlaski, who lived in a house in the garden of what is now Number 12 South Bailey, not the house on the Wear's bend known as Count's House. He died in 1937 at the age of 98. The monument reads: 'Near this spot repose the remains of Count

Joseph Borowlaski, a native of Pokucia in the late kingdom of Poland. This extraordinary man measured no more than three feet three inches in height but his form was well proportioned.' The Count was renowned for being both a dandy and bad tempered. One story has it that his wife, who was over 6 foot tall, used to pick him up during outbursts and sit him on the mantelpiece. The monument appears to have been intended for the cathedral but ended in the church of the parish in which he lived and died.

The original reredos, from the cathedral, was made of black oak, originally Elizabethan. The sculpture in Hartlepool stone above the vestry door is 12th century and depicts Christ in ascension with the symbols of the four Evangelists in the four corners. This used to belong to St Giles's Church.

Successive principals have had to alter the building for its continued use as the college chapel. In 1924, under Wallis, it was 'greatly beautified, being reseated and refurnished, the old organ removed from the chancel [following a generous donation from the vice-principal, P.R. Frost], and a new electrically blown organ installed at the west end'. R.R. Williams's alterations were more substantial, including the addition of electric light, replacing oil lamps, and the opening of the Norman chancel arch by the

The chapel interior from the organ gallery. Substantial renovations and improvements were carried out during 2002 to adapt the building to the growing college's needs, and restoring the layout closely to the buildings 12th century appearance. Alterations included floor levelling, under floor heating new lighting and adaptable seating. The cost of around £230,000 included significant donations from alumni, trusts, staff, and friends of St John's.

Sundays at St John's

'The Sunday morning 8am communion was the great service of the week in the college chapel. It was strictly 1662 (of course) with hymns and a sermon by a member of staff. All were expected to be there. Breakfast followed and a leisured interval until it was time to go to the cathedral – dressed properly in gowns – for matins, which was then the main service of the day – no choral communions then! The sermon would be worth hearing, for there was a galaxy of fine preachers in Durham– Michael Ramsey, Dean Alington, Alan Richardson. Sunday dinner was the best meal of the week, with a roast. Then a stroll – maybe through Houghall Woods or, for those amorously inclined, to Mary's or Hild's. Tea, with or without ladies, was well prepared by a visit to the cake shops on Saturday morning and was quite an event. We then went to evensong. And after cold supper – the worst meal of the week – it was SCM or DICCU, or sometimes a student service at St Mary-le-Bow. Members of the diploma group (later known as Cranmer Hall) needed to have their amorous teas on Saturday, for they would be walking down to the bus station in mid-afternoon for the journey to one of the outlying colliery villages, where, in one of the tin tabernacles provided for the miners, they would practise the art of preaching and service-taking at destinations such as

Newfield, Byers Green, Billy Row. The people rather liked the young men from college, in spite of their sermons, and would prepare them for the service by an enormous tea before the blazing fire in one of the miner's cottages. Fortified in this way, Mrs Gadd's cold supper didn't much matter! It was a well-filled Sunday, and a good preparation for the Sunday programme that most of the 1940s ordinands would have to face when they went to their first parishes.'

Leslie Stanbridge (ordinand 1947–50, chaplain 1951–5)

Wallis Organ Scholarship

Principal Wallis's renowned love of music, particularly the piano, is reflected in his endowment of the Wallis Organ Scholarship, which celebrates its 64th anniversary in the college's centenary year. The scholarship grew out of the money given to Principal Wallis on his retirement. In 1975, when the new undergraduate chapel became the library, the old organ was removed and the new organ was put in a newly constructed organ loft. The organ, built in 1963 by Harrison & Harrison of Durham with 11 stops over two manuals and pedals, is typical of its time – loud and piercing – and since it was not revoiced for its new setting it is rather too loud for the chapel. A complete replacement is currently being considered at the time of writing.

The Wallis Organ Scholarship [worth £300 per annum with an additional £150 for lessons] has been offered for several years to a student at the university. The role of the scholar has changed considerably in recent years, from essentially that of a parish organist, accompanying hymns and very occasional anthems, to a semi-professional post similar to those offered by Oxbridge colleges. This change has been brought about mostly due to the influence of Dr Stephen Hampton, former senior tutor, by whose insistence the college offered first eight, in 2004, and then, from 2005, 16 choral scholarships, and a director of the choral scholars, a post held for the last three years by George Richford. With the choral scholarships the college found itself in the enviable position of having the finest chapel choir in the university and the only one in which all of its members were auditioned and are paid. Naturally, the standard of music is now extremely high, and as Organ Scholar I have accompanied the choir every week at evensong, toured with the choir and recorded a cd (published under the Guild label in 2008). A new post of Assistant Organ Scholar has become necessary from 2008 as the choir continues to flourish and sing more frequently. The choir now sings compline on Sunday evenings in addition to evensong on Wednesdays. I have been extremely fortunate to be the Organ Scholar at St John's during this time, as the music has been of a very high standard and the role very involved. I have also, somewhat unusually, been the Scholar for three years. George has been the director for the same period, and this continuity has allowed the choir to continue to improve year on year.

Lawrence Tao (Wallis Organ Scholar 2005–8)

removal of the rood screen. The original furniture was replaced to allow more space for students, and the pews were replaced by 'collegiate style' three-stepped rows.

Nowadays, 'college chapel' does not just mean worship in St Mary-the-Less; many services are held in Leech Hall, although with the renovations completed in 2005, the worship space available is much more adaptable. There has even been a theatrical performance of *Dr Faustus* in 2007 'in the round'. Just as the 'spirit' of St John's continues, so does the work of the 'heart' of the college: worship, prayer and praise throughout each week.

Finance

St John's Hall was initially generously supported by significant gifts from William D. Cruddas, who donated £5,000 for the purchase of Bowes House (then Haughton House). This was followed by a second £5,000 for the building of Cruddas House in 1912–13 (worth over £215,000 today). However, St John's only just kept its head above water financially. As early as April 1913 Principal Dawson-Walker called for supporters to make substantial endowments both for the establishment of the hall and scholarships, bursaries and exhibitions. By the 1920s six significant bursaries had developed, in addition to two Jesmond exhibitions of £40 a year and the Ratford-Bromley Prize.

A number of scholarships, prizes and bursaries are available from St John's College in 2008, including:

- The Wallis Organ Scholarship, which recognizes ability and secures the services of an organist for the college chapel.
- The Scholarship Fund, which provides access awards, in-course bursaries and personal development awards to support students to make the best of their time at the university, who might otherwise struggle financially or be prevented from accessing all the opportunities available, or to fund a postgraduate scholarship with a geographic bias toward the developing world with a theology and ministry focus.
- The SCR Travel Bursary.
- The Million Shilling Fund, which aims to support the religious education of evangelical students at St John's college, particularly the children of clergy.

- The Bowron Bursary Fund, which is a travel bursary for relief work for the poor in India.
- The St John's Student Opportunities Fund, which offers grants for the relief of hardship and monies to enable participation and enrichment.
- The Cranmer Visiting Fellowship Fund and the Raymond Dew Fellowship, which exist to develop St John's reputation in research.

THE BURSAR'S TALE

Robert Scott-Biggs (Bursar 1995–2003) reflects on the Bursar's function at St John's College: 'The role of bursar can be an uncomfortable one, requiring as it often does the diplomatic skills of a Henry Kissinger combined with a hide like a rhinoceros. The main responsibility of the role has in the past been to send out student bills and ensure prompt collection. Because the skills required to carry out this function successfully have been perceived to be order, discipline and ability as an efficient administrator, it has been the practice to recruit bursars from the ranks of the retired military. In 1995 three of the Durham University colleges' bursars were ex-military. However, with the requirement that educational institutions have a more business focus, the role of bursar has become that of a business manager, with an emphasis on cost-effective resource management combined with a keen sense for financial strategy. The bursar's responsibility is also to identify creative ways through which the resources necessary to support the work of education can be provided, such as conferences, catering functions and property lettings.

Fees, 1920

In 1920 fees were inclusive of university tuition, one university exam a year, subscriptions to all university and college sports clubs, board and lodging, tuition in college and medical treatment. For arts and theology students this was: £110.15.0 [equivalent to around £2,400 today]; For science students this was: £116.15.0 [equivalent to around £2,500 today].
In 2008, the annual fee is £12,825 (£4,275 per term), including all the above.

Bursar Robert Scott-Biggs.

'The 21st-century student has high expectations, not only for their degree course but for the facilities provided by the institution (such as en-suite residential accommodation and good food). The provision and maintenance of such facilities come at a very high price.

'The independent nature of St John's College is the source of the unique challenge of having to serve two masters. As both a university college and a ministry training organization, a delicate balance and distinction between these two functions is essential. Success in meeting these challenges is dependent on the extent to which the key values of the college translate into realistic strategies that support its continuation. The evangelical Christian ethos with its practical emphasis on care for the individual and good stewardship of the God-given resources should be the foundation from which the institution develops and grows. The bursar's role is fundamental in ensuring that this process continues.'

FINANCIAL REVIEW 2008

Campbell Grant (Bursar since 2003) reflects on the current situation: 'I knew both previous Bursars – Robert Scott-Biggs and John Hirst – in Tonbridge, Kent, in the 1980s. Do all bursars come from there? One of the main features of being a bursar is the breadth of tasks: I have responsibilities for governance (as company secretary), finance, human resources, estates, catering, housekeeping, vacation business, IT, legislative compliance, environment, the college bar, even the crèche.

Through careful cost control and increased charges, St John's capacity to generate funds for reinvestment in capital works is improving towards 5 per cent and thus spend on capital works – which has annually been of the order of £200,000 range in recent years – can increase in order to fund better accommodation, and ordination training.'

A SHORT HISTORY OF DEVELOPMENT APPEALS

Initially St John's Hall was established with a capital of only £2 (worth around £115 in today's money). The generous support of William Cruddas enabled the purchase of College's first buildings (Bowes and Haughton Houses) and the building of Cruddas House in 1912. Despite this, even as early as 1913 Principal Dawson-Walker called for endowments for the establishment of the hall and scholarships, bursaries and exhibitions. In 2008 the scholarships, prizes or bursaries provided by St John's, fully supported by the Joint Junior Common Room, Senior Common Room and St John's Society, included: The Scholarship Fund (incorporating The Wallis Organ Scholarship and enabling access to opportunities); the Senior Common Room Travel Bursary; the Million Shilling Fund, to support the education of, particularly, the children of clergy; the Bowron Bursary Fund, the travel bursary for relief work in India; the Student Opportunities Fund; the Cranmer Visiting Fellowship Fund and the Raymond Dew Fellowship (for research); the Young Christian Authors' Workshop; and the Fellow in Preaching and Apologetics.

Dora Cruddas

After William Cruddas, his eldest daughter, Dora, was St John's most significant benefactor and a 'staunch friend' to the college. On the occasion of her death in 1929 the following tribute was paid to her by Principal Wallis: 'She contributed very largely to the fund for purchasing the building known as Haughton House [among other endowments]. Her handsome legacy of £20,000 [now worth over £650,000] will ensure the financial stability of the college.' She also gave money for bursaries and exhibitions. 'For the last five years I have regularly spent some days each year at Haughton Castle to enable her to have a close, intimate knowledge of St John's men, of what had been accomplished each year, of our ideals and our needs and hopes for the future. It was characteristic of her that she should study the annual college group closely, asking personal questions about individual men – that she should keep her own book of photographs up to date, desiring me always to supply her with fresh copies – that she should follow the careers of past students with keenness – that she should discuss

with me the times of strain in college life and should ask me to pray with her for the college and its work. [Her interest was] something personal, intimate and keen.'

The Cruddas' ancestral home, Haughton Castle, after which number 3 South Bailey is now named.

A £70,000 Jubilee Appeal was launched between 1959–69 to build Cranmer Hall's new block. The following 1972–4 Appeal aimed to raise £125,000 to refurbish buildings. Lionel Holmes assisted Principal Cockerton with this appeal: 'We drove to some 45 meetings held all over the country. We took a map of the British Isles, which I had stuck with coloured pins representing where Old Johnians lived, topped with the rather vacuous heading "How dense are the OJs?" The sum total of alumni alive at that time was only about 1500 [in 2008 they number over 4500] Some of the meetings were graced by quite prominent people, including the then Archbishop of York, Donald Coggan (on the college council). It was a fascinating experience.'

From 1985, under alumnus Adrian Beney, St John's was the first college to establish a dedicated development office, a pattern later followed by the university. He remembers: 'Four years and

£625,000 later we had a new Leech Hall, refurbished rooms, and restored stonework along the Bailey. Hard work, the dedicated support of Nigel Sherlock and Harry Taylor [amongst others, including J. Derek Hodgson and Iain Mulholland] brought in an unprecedented sum to the college. Prayer meetings were held, old furniture sold at auction, the entire governing body gave, as did a remarkable number of the JCR members; there was a real team spirit to it at times.'

More recently, the development fund has flourished under the guidance of Jane Grieve and Lois Stuckenbruck, amongst others, raising £1 million for College projects including a community worker in Gateshead, the Sam Kermu Fellowship and Alphonce Mphaphi Mohapi Scholarship. Since 2000 another £1 million has been raised for projects including: a new boathouse, renewing student internet access, the Centre For Biblical Literacy and the St John's Student Opportunities Fund.

I would sum up the spirit of St John's as 'civilized, with a lively Christian faith.'

Campbell Grant, bursar since 2003

PART 3

Student Life

Student Life through the Century

Each student's idea of how St John's should be is shaped by the routine and style of student life as it was when they were there: the standard of accommodation, the scholarly standards and commitments, the social calendar and so on. What remains unchanged is the sense of community and the underpinning Christian ethos of the college, small enough to feel like 'home' and 'family'.

'Student life' is such a subjective term, so difficult to summarize. Of course, many student events are impromptu, or not recorded other than by memory, so it has been difficult to provide anything but an impressionistic view of college life. Material which remains in the archive shows that 'Johnsmen' were expected to be gentleman scholars. Their routine now appears strict, but allowances were made for afternoon tea every day.

A 1924 prospectus outlines the requirements: students took lectures at the university in their degree or diploma courses (theology, arts, science or education), in addition to four college lectures each week (tutors were trained in classics, Hebrew and biblical subjects).

At the time a great number of theological 'heavyweights' taught theology, including Canon Professor Oliver Quick, A.E.J. Rawlinson and A.M. Ramsey. There was a small college library in what is now the Tristram Room, but most books were in the university library on Palace Green. George Parkinson (1944–7) remembers that: 'All lectures were at Palace Green, or sometimes in selected colleges, and the main library for the university was what is now the law library on Palace Green.'

H. Wilkinson remembers: 'Life in St John's was somewhat different from what it is today … We had, of course, no bar. One could buy cigarettes from the butler. It was said of him, and he was a man we all respected, that you knew what he thought of a student if he referred to him either with or without the prefix "Mr". We were given one smallish bucket of coal for our fires each day. One irritating "economy" was that each night at about

Leslie Stanbridge (right) remembers St John's in the 1940s as a 'gentlemanly place'.

Henry Ganderton

A reflection of the 'spirit' of St John's could be seen in the number of former students who return as staff members, and none more so than Henry Ganderton, who held a variety of posts in college between 1913 and 1929.

Henry Yorke Ganderton came to St John's to study for a BA Litt.Ant. in 1913, 'a student full of life and pranks', and left to be a sailor involved in the Battle of Jutland. He returned as 'a sober-minded "theolog"', including Senior Man in 1919, to be awarded the Diploma in Theology in 1920 and then a master's degree. After his ordination as deacon in 1920 he was chaplain for the next nine years. He was also bursar (1921–9) and vice-principal (1924–9), and became affectionately known as Gandy. 'Ganderton, now vice-principal and bursar, renders excellent service in many departments

outside his two official ones. His influence is felt for good in many quarters, and his sane outlook is of very great value. In sports, of course, he continues to be an enthusiastic supporter of the boats [as cox and secretary of UDBC].' He left St John's in 1929 to become headmaster of Durham Choristers' School.

He was fond of photography. The grandson of the college's butler, Dennison, remembers seeing him on the riverbanks in the dark taking pictures of the recently flood-lit cathedral in the 1950s or 1960s. He preached regularly at St Margaret's Church, Crossgate, and in 1947 he was made a canon of Durham Cathedral. He died in 1975, and his memorial service was held during cathedral evensong on 25 October.

The quotations are from Wallis' appreciation of Ganderton in *Old Johnian*, 1926 and 1929

10.30 the principal switched off all the lights at the mains, thus those who stayed up late did so with candles [or oil lamps] …

James Atkinson remembers that in the mid-1930s he was allowed a bucket of coal a day for his fire in his Cruddas room, and he recalls often managing to save up coal from the day before.

The cathedral and its music and preaching made a great impression on many undergraduates. For James Atkinson it was 'Anglican worship at its best'. Bishop Hensley Henson was a wonderful preacher, who gave 'superb orations'. Leslie Stanbridge (1947–50) remembers that services in the cathedral were attended in 'full regalia, gowns flying'.

James Atkinson remembers the 'gentle rivalry' between John's and Chad's, who were known as 'Chad's cads'. In the 1950s the relationship between John's and Chad's was marked by 'warm friendliness and cooperation punctuated by occasional rags' (Williams's memoirs, quoted in Yates, p.41), sharing the range of Anglican churchmanship. Leslie Stanbridge, among others, remembers 'sport' between Johnsmen and Chadsmen in the winter of 1957: Chad's held their annual dinner with the Bishop of Durham as their distinguished guest. Johnsmen walled up Chad's front door with frozen ice blocks from the river so the only way out was down the riverbanks. John Hunter remembers that 'an indignant principal of Chad's had to ring R.R. Williams to be let out!' R.R. was unable to find any students.

Leslie Stanbridge (1947–50) remembers St John's as a 'very good college, very closely knit' during the 1940s and 1950s. It was

'a broadening place' where 'we had quite good fun one way or another … Durham was a wonderful place for characters'. (After two years in a south London parish he returned to college as chaplain in 1951 following a personal request from R.R. Williams.)

Throughout the early 20th century the university's Officers' Training Corps 'provided undergraduates with a standardized measure of elementary military training' at headquarters at No. 3 Queen Street. Durham University Corps were taken on camp for annual training in the summer vacation. In the roll of service for 1914–19 988 students were listed as serving members of the Durham University Officer Training Corps.

Failure to wear undergraduate gowns meant being reprimanded by the university policemen. Alan Clark remembers that even in the 1960s 'gowns were worn at all times during the academic day, not an imposition during the Durham winter, when every additional item of clothing was welcome. However, gowns had to be worn on top of all other clothing, including waterproofs in wet weather and failure to comply attracted the attention of the officers. I look at photographs of college friends in the early 1960s with disbelief. Could we all have worn shirts (mostly white) and ties with blazers or Harris Tweed jackets as our daily attire?'

Cecily Williams, wife of Principal Williams (1945–54), joined in wholeheartedly with student life. 'I was invited to every college event that I cared to attend. I went to debates and to coffee parties, I applauded from the touchline at the soccer

Items Required by Students

In the 1930s students were required to bring with them the following items, which 'were to be observed as a condition of membership':

- their own bed linen, including two pairs single-sided sheets, two pillowcases and towels; all marked with own name
- a dark coat
- a gown; 'black stuff gowns of the correct university shape may be obtained from Greys & Son in Durham, Ede & Ravenscroft in Chancery Lane, London, or Wippell & Son in Charing Cross, London'
- a 'small outfit' for tea, including a kettle, cups and saucers

Ordinary necessary furniture is provided for each student's room, 'but it is customary for a student to have his own pictures, cushions, etc.' Items suggested in the 2002 prospectus included:

- kettle, coffee, tea, sugar, biscuits
- hi-fi and music
- corkscrews x 2 (one will be lost or stolen)
- glasses, mug, plates, cutlery (for impromptu late-night cook-ups, dinner parties)
- fancy dress (school uniform, etc.)
- evening wear (dj, dress, etc.)
- big warm duvet, sheets and lots of pillows
- videos/DVDs (the video room is a very comfortable place to spend a cheap night in)
- washing powder

Nixon's tall, Painter's short, Yates is, Prin was.

from 1967–8 JCR food book

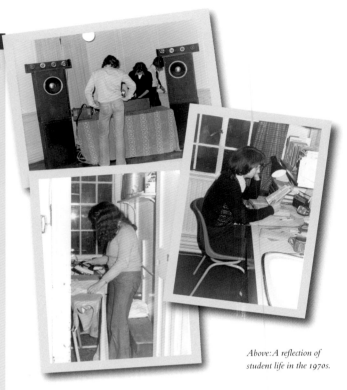

Above: A reflection of student life in the 1970s.

8th June 1967, 3am. Geoff Howard, one of 'The Phantom Dauber' team, painting out yellow parking lines outside St Mary-the-Less.

matches, and I tore up and down the towpath yelling for John's in the boat races ... At the end of the Michaelmas term there was always the carol service in chapel, the Christmas dinner in hall and the college concert, which was almost the best event of the year. The staff learned exactly what the students thought of them and Wesky [our dog] made an annual and popular appearance in each one. The Lent term brought the boat race and the 'flu epidemics, and the Trinity term included the college hike immediately before June Week.'

John Oliver (1950–5) remembers: 'There was a nine-something curfew for those of us who lived "outside", cheerfully ignored. And a judicious throwing of a small stone at the right window would soon see a locked door open, though it was reported that on one occasion a student managed to hit the principal's [Williams's] window. Ladies were not allowed in our rooms "after tea" (similar rules observed in other colleges). When my fiancée came up to Durham she came back to my room for coffee one evening. As we exited the front door at 10 pm we received a loud and cheery greeting from the college chaplain (Barzillai Beckerleg), which was a welcome sign that adults could be responsible. Another irksome rule was that no alcohol was allowed in college – the only dry college in Durham.'

Winters in Durham could be particularly harsh, particularly the winters of the 1960s. J.D.S. Clark (1961–4) says: 'I remember the winter of 1963 with the Bailey frozen over for two months,

William Maurice lecturing in Greek c1974

Various Memories from the 1970s

'A college tie looking vaguely Wagnerian with menacing eagles. Striped scarves looking like vertical bruises, black and blue. Old copies of college regulations banning alcohol, women and electricity consumption. Love letters, coffee cups, soup-stained gowns, garments dyed or melted in your skirmish with the college laundry facilities. Sounds from a College Ball, a phrase or two from a College sermon. That frantic silence in the library before exams. Pious noises from DICCU prayer meetings while others played Led Zepplin full blast. The taste of College food, the tang of Newky Brown... In my day the facilities certainly didn't make it memorable. No bar, food so meagre we used to play a game called 'spot the meat'... Perhaps it had most to do with the kind of ethos that's always been so integral to the College tradition. John's has been a community trying to live out a Christian, ethical and educational vision. 'Fides nostra victoria' is, if you like a statement of purpose for a unique educational establishment.'

Adrian Dorber, former JCR President,
St John's Society speech, June 1998

shutters on Eden [Haughton] House windows closed, and buckets of coal sneaked from the cellar ... students in duffel coats with hoods up, like medieval monks.'

Alan Clark, who was at St John's in the early 1960s, remembers other aspects of college life: 'My principal college expense, after books, was laundry. We all had our bedding and personal laundry collected each week from the college and returned in neat parcels of string-tied brown paper. ... In those days there was no college bar, and no television either in our rooms or the JCR. With formal dinner each evening not finishing until 7.30 or later, we either went off to university activities or retired to one of our rooms for coffee and talk for the rest of the evening, essay duties permitting. At one stage compline was said in one of our rooms to conclude the evening.'

The 1999 yearbook tells of 'one raucous end of year formal in the heady 1960s, the principal [Hickinbotham] delivered his after-dinner speech. "What we need in this college," he intoned, "is a birdbath." No one noticed a small group of John's students sneak out by the backdoor. By midnight, Haughton lawn was covered with 14 deluxe birdbaths from the surrounding neighbourhood.'

Richard Adams (1965–8) didn't take student life entirely seriously: 'In 1966 thanks to stream-tracing chemicals from ICI for our "geological expedition to Iceland" we'd dyed the Wear red on the main day of the Regatta; painted the police TV and traffic

A highlight of Christmas pantomimes are the staff's costumes and demonstration of theatrical 'talents'. Here, tutor Gillian Boughton relishes her role in a 1970s production held in Haughton dining room.

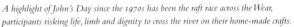

A highlight of John's Day since the 1970s has been the raft race across the Wear, participants risking life, limb and dignity to cross the river on their home-made crafts.

days. The rugby-playing Dafydd Jones used to be heard every morning from about 6:30 onwards singing Welsh songs extremely loudly in the shower and in his room.'

According to Phil Thomas, 'John's really is a unique university experience, and while students' experiences over the last 100 years will have differed wildly, I believe that the atmosphere and inclusive spirit of college is what binds alumni together. Abiding memories: long summer evenings on Linton Lawn, the crowd around the quiz machine in the Bailey Room, the late-night cups of tea and chats, freshers' week 2002 and

control booth in the marketplace; frequently removed most of the food for next day's breakfast from the college kitchens.'

The year 1967 saw St John's first entry in the Guinness Book of Records: a student called Newel ate 104 prunes in 11 minutes and 2.1 seconds.

Richard Horton (1983–6) remembers: 'That first term was intensely lived and scored its impressions deeply. It was a heady time, one of many firsts, of friendships formed, and of discovering a completely new way of life. St Johns, as has been amply demonstrated by Catherine Fox's [Cathy Wilcox] "tell-it-as-it-is" novels [particularly *Angels and Men* (1995)] is not exactly a normal college, and its particular mix of the religious and secular gives it a very distinctive atmosphere.'

Georgina Wilczek (née Luck, 1995–9) writes: 'A highlight of my first year was Ed Shaw's doughnut tea parties, which he held each week in his room at the end of Linton Wing, the smallest room in college! There were a lot of water fights all down the corridors, especially on Linton Wing and Linton B floor. This did not go down well because the electrics would end up soaked and we would be banned from turning on the lights for a couple of

The unique Linton B24a (left and below) in 1997 and Victoria B, room 2 in 1998. The editor's home from home a decade ago. Note the lack of computer!

Student Numbers	
1909	5
1912	40
1918	12
1919	50
1921	58
1926	62
1939	78
1945	12
1948	12
1953	108
1954	100
1963	147
1969	207
1976	246
1977	307
2008	353

getting up at stupid o'clock to run in my gown, the raft race on John's Day and trying to avoid being swept down the Wear while avoiding eggs being thrown from the bank, the college grounds when it had snowed, going to breakfast at 8 am after my final summer ball, and, above all, the relationships that formed in September 2002 that still mean a huge amount now.'

In 1995 David Day noted: 'What strikes me about John's and Cranmer students is their energy, their generosity, their exhausting *joie de vivre*, their goodwill and friendliness. And among many of the very bright, very privileged, very talented young people I encounter a sense that they want to give something back. I know that sounds unbelievably corny but talk to them and see if you don't agree.'

Of course, times change quickly. The college is not the same today as it was even ten years ago. Adrian Vincent remembers: 'My period, 1990–93, was at the turning-point before irreversible change to student life. Everyone was guaranteed a place to live in St John's on the Bailey for all three years if they wanted; those who lived "out" tended to gravitate back to St John's for much of their social life. The result was that I knew the names of all the undergraduates in all three years, and the majority of those in my year I classed as friends rather than acquaintances. Only a couple of students had mobile phones, and few had their own computer, so rather than communicating by email, mobile or text, you simply walked round to someone's room to see if they were in. If they were not – a bit of a chore if you had walked half an hour to Hild–Bede or Aidan's – you would simply write an amusing message on the pad of paper they had on their door and then see if someone else was in

Amabel Craig writes: 'I remember a spate of fire alarms in 1997. We became so accustomed to being disturbed by the unnerving sound of the alarm that we left our shoes and coat by the door to get ready quickly. There were at least ten alarm calls in that first term. Virtually all were hoaxes, traced to a disgruntled "liver-out".

'Emails were starting to become more common when I arrived in 1997, but were still a novelty.

'I also remember the novelty of mobile phones in college in 1997. Only a few people owned them, and were ridiculed slightly for owning and using them. They were further impaired by the poor reception in college. Of course, most of us used the pay-phones scattered around college. We all seemed to have a phone card, which reversed the call charges to our parents. On a recent visit to college I noticed that the pay-phones had gone. Presumably all students have their own mobiles, and reception has improved!'

All contributors have been enthusiastic about St John's sense of community and the importance of the Christian ethos, despite the broadening of the college's make-up. Our victory is still found in faith. One alumnus summarizes John's life as 'Simply the Best!' It is the community of St John's that remains constant. As a college it is small enough to feel like home, a family, and as Howard 'the Bedel' Stevens says: 'We have 'em for three years then turf them out into the wild blue yonder. And we love 'em. We couldn't do what we do if the college was any bigger. It has been a privilege to work here. It is a place of atmosphere and love.'

Top: Students enjoying unusually good weather at John's Day, July 2008.
Above: Roald Dahl themed bar night, 2003.

The Junior Common Room

St John's is a unique college in that it has three subsidiary common rooms: the Junior, Middle (established in 2004) and Cranmer Hall Common Rooms, each with its own constitution and annual elections. The JCR President is non-sabbatical.

The Junior Common Room was established in the 1950s with the stipulation that the Senior Man was to be an undergraduate in his final year before entering Cranmer Hall. The introduction of women to Cranmer Hall in 1966 and John's Hall in 1973 raised such thorny constitutional issues that 'the women' were referred to as 'honorary gentlemen' for a time!

Neil Robinson remembers his time as Senior Man in 1953–4: 'The appointment of Senior Man in my day was made by the Principal, no doubt after consultation. I saw the Senior Man's job as and when necessary representing the staff to the students and vice versa. It was a "nuts and bolts" job trying to ensure that people and events fitted easily and comfortably together. There was much appreciation, kindness, support and good humour in a job that I must admit I did not find onerous. Representing the college as invited for "state" occasions was always a pleasure and a considerable honour.'

More recently, Chris Morris (President 1999–2000) remembers: 'My highlights were when John's students took an active part in university and college life. That tradition of involvement [in wider issues] has long been a Johnian strength. My experience as President was the first time I'd seen so

James Major (JCR President 1998–9) and David Day. James remembers: 'It was a year in which the JCR enjoyed excellent relations with the other parts of college which together created a positive and relaxed atmosphere in college enabling significant changes to the fabric of the building and helped to deal with the various crises that inevitably arose. What strikes me most about John's is what a fantastically friendly place it was and still is.'

many people, with different goals, ambitions, personalities, disagreements and so on all coming together to form such a strong community. I've not seen anything like it since.'

The Joint JCR has reflected the student body's concern over social issues; of particular note is the matter of policy over fair trade produce supplied throughout college (ratified in 1998), building upon fair trade concerns epitomized by the Nestlé boycott in place since 1978.

JCR Presidents Becca Davies (2007–8) and Martin Hodgetts (2008–9) at a John's vs Cranmer rugby match, March 2008.

Sporting Life

Although St John's is one of the smallest colleges in Durham, in many sporting areas it 'punches above its weight'. Principal Hickinbotham took pleasure in reporting that, in 1965, St John's 'continues to play what is for almost the smallest college a very active part in the athletic, cultural and social life of the university' (*Durham Johnian*, 1965).

H. S. Wilkinson, an undergraduate in the 1920s, cites this as a personal advantage: 'I, for example, with no previous experience of rowing, would not have received the careful and painstaking coaching which I received and which gave me many happy and healthy hours on the river.' Neil Robinson (1947–54, Senior Man 1953–4) says: 'At St John's, if you were keen on sport you were expected to do everything. We were not memorable as athletes in St John's!' Of course, the sporting successes or failures of particular years depend on the current intake, and the staff member responsible for admissions (currently, the senior tutor) has a large – often conscious – part to play in this.

Johnians have always taken advantage of a wide variety of sports. A 1914 prospectus lists the following: rowing, cricket, association football, hockey, lawn tennis, athletics: 'each with a honourable record and high standard to maintain.' In order to participate in such sports, students had to pay 10 shillings a term.

Introduced later were fencing, table tennis and hockey. Notable sportsmen frequently mentioned in Johnian dispatches were E. Dawson-Walker (son of Principal Dawson-Walker), C.K. Pattinson, E.W.P. Ainsworth and L.H. Rhodes.

In 1988 the alumni newsletter, *Fides*, mentions the following sports: volleyball, hockey, rugby success (men); football, alongside netball (the sport of queens, according to the 1997 yearbook), squash and cricket. Other sports currently participated in by college members include darts, golf, snowboarding, tiddlywinks and, of course, pool, evidenced by four college teams (including a women's team) rotating around the table in the JCR.

FIVES

The year 1957 was a 'most successful season' for fives. The college club won all matches, including against Durham School and Bede and Hatfield Colleges. The team included John Hancock (captain), Ian Hogg, Brian Crosby and Allen Reutter (Hancock and Hogg were university players). St John's won the fives trophy (for the first time in the trophy's 63 years) by the greatest margin for many years. It is assumed that matches were played at Ushaw College. Because the game is now played less in schools, it is no longer played at Durham University.

Colours First Won

- Association Football – December 1913;
- Hockey – March 1913
- Athletics – May 1914
- Cricket – June 1914
- Tennis – June 1914
- Rugby Football – January 1922
- Fives – March 1933 December 1937 (half);
- Swimming – December 1936

Cheering on Johnian rowing teams on the riverbanks, c.1920s.

RUGBY AND FOOTBALL

John Oliver (1950–5) remembers his time as rugby captain. He was the only player with prior experience and recollects the team's 'triumph' when John's was beaten by Bede College (then a PE college) only 15–3; the usual score was about 50–5!

Phil Thomas (2002–6) writes: 'Rugby demanded an altogether different level of commitment [from football]. I still wince at memories of my first training session in January 2003. It was one of those grey winter afternoons at Maiden Castle where the wind whips in through however many layers of clothing you wear. The main training drill involved two players at a time doing circuits of the infamous hill, followed by running 50 metres up the steepest point and hitting a tackle bag. Truth be told, these were difficult times for John's rugby, with only a small core of committed players, of whom Richard Lister and Andrew Schofield deserve special mention. The two years of their captaincies and a good intake of freshers meant that during 2005–6 we achieved a pretty rare feat of an unbeaten season, with a 40–0 triumph over Hatfield (their B team admittedly, but no one need know that)! The player of the year that season was my ex-roommate James Davies, who combined the Incredible Hulk with Road Runner.'

John's vs Cranmer rugby match, 12 March 2008.

St John's 1933 Rugby team.

In the 1912–13 season most matches were won, and in the 1913–14 season St John's came top of all the colleges, losing only one match. In 1914 football at John's was described as 'particularly strong'.

Phil Thomas (2002–6) remembers: 'My main memories of football concerned the then [JCR] president Tim Woodall. It was his tackle that arrived about eight seconds late that resulted in a penalty and brought on a minor blip in the first game of the 2002–3 season (we shipped ten goals in about half an hour to lose 11–1), which set the tone for the majority of the season – the mantra was often "we won that if you don't count the first ten minutes", but the spirit of the team lived on, and results gradually improved to the point where we led Trevelyan B 3–2 going into injury time in the penultimate game of the season. A relatively successful season justified all the team-building Wednesday lunches in The Swan and Three pub.'

Football is not the preserve of the male members of college Ruth Curry recalls. 'I was women's football captain at John's for the 2001–2 season. It was a great season, probably their most successful in recent history, despite many of the girls never having kicked a ball before! Within no time (and thanks to coaches Ross Armstrong and Richard 'Dickie' Allen) we had a super regular first team who won every match (but two) during the year, finishing a close second in the league and gaining promotion to the premier league.' At the 2002 Epiphany Awards Ball, all the members of the team were awarded half or full colours for sport.

LAWN TENNIS

The 1914 prospectus describes lawn tennis as being 'well to the fore'. Tutor J.H. Wadsworth (1909–19) was remembered as a keen tennis player and must have supported the college team. In 1911

1913 Tennis Team.

Playing cricket on Linton Lawn, Principal Sykes caught out!

St John's was 'undoubtedly the strongest in the university'. More recently, however, 1957–8 was a poor season and 'we could not even beat St Chad's!'

CRICKET

St John's first victory against Hatfield College was in 1910, and by the following year, college boasted 'a really good XI with some victories'. In 1913, according to the 1914 prospectus, St John's played in the final for the Grey Cup in which all Durham constituent colleges played.

In the 1960s St John's won the cricket trophy twice in three years, and Timothy Yates, tutor then warden, remembers that in the 1970s: 'I played cricket for both the university staff side and for the diocese: I still have a piece of paper showing Will Stewart, myself and John Painter heading the batting averages for the university staff side! Will must have been recruited to make up numbers. To the delight of Canon Frank Chase, the diocese won the Church Times cup in 1965: he was a Durham graduate. Paul Conder, John Painter and myself all played regularly for the side.' In 1974 St John's won the cricket trophy again.

The 1913 Cricket Club.

Phil Thomas (2002–6) writes: 'Games of Linton Lawn cricket sprang up regularly from March onwards each year. Just like cricket – but with the advantage of requiring no ability or technique – these games reached their peak in the post-exams period when 20 or 30 people (boys and girls – it was always a very egalitarian game!) at a time could join in. Even "The Bish" [Principal Stephen Sykes] made an appearance on occasion – it probably says something about my sporting ability that catching him out represents one of the high points of my college sporting career!'

ATHLETICS AND CROSS-COUNTRY

In May 1914 St John's won the college team race trophy, but by 1958 it was reported that 'there [did] not seem to be enough enthusiasm for athletics in the college, and a revival would seem therefore to be clearly indicated' (Nial Meredith and David Towne in *Durham Johnian*).

There has been a recent resurgence in cross-country. Matt Giles (2003–8) remembers: 'I was privileged enough to be involved in our recent cross-country successes, for two of which I was captain. These team photos [are] from the two races of our 2005 season, during which we won the intercollegiate competition for the seventh successive year and thus were able to keep the trophy permanently – in return we gave the university cross-country club a new trophy named after Principal Sykes. To celebrate these successes a framed scroll was commissioned and is now in the college entrance. The women's team have also done well, winning the very first women's intercollegiate race in 2003. We have had unrivalled support (with someone asking if it was

Sporting Memories

'On the sporting side the croquet marathon that was held on Cranmer lawn and built a world record and thus was included in the *Guinness Book of Records*; rowing training, which involved circuits and early-morning river outings – wonderful on a sunny day in summer, but not so great in the winter – the patience of our cox Tim and excitement and extreme nervousness of taking part in our first competitive regatta [as the first female rowing team from St John's]. The hockey games – we were not very good really but we did represent the college! I guess this was what life at John's was all about, students with a sense of community spirit who lived and worked together over three short years, which flew so quickly.' (Charlotte South (née Owen), 1973–6).

Johnians at Durham Regatta c.1920.

St John's university at the Cathedral Relays in 2004!).' To celebrate this success, college members wore a blue hoody with 'Chariots of Fire' quote and a red hoody with 'Magnificent Seven' design.

As Principal Sykes said: 'It is difficult to explain why the second smallest college in the university should field, for seven years in a row, the university's best four cross–country runners. Equally notable, for this anniversary occasion, were the unprecedented numbers of members of college cheering on – no fewer than 27 – John's runners' (*College Record, 2006*).

ROWING

St John's has always had a good reputation for rowing, and the college enjoyed many years of success on the water. Of course, this, as with other sports, depends on the strength and experience of college members. Certain members of staff have played significant roles in this, particularly Henry Ganderton in the 1910s and 1920s as boat club captain, cox and coach, both as undergraduate and tutor. Stephen Hampton (senior tutor 2004–7) paid particular

attention to applicants' mention of sport on university application form and developed a good team of sporting Johnians.

In October 1910 the college held a trial for a four-oared boat. Johnsmen took part in all intercollegiate races, and would a few years later in 1914 boast two boats in the river. The boathouse was built in 1911 with a substantial donation from the Revd Watts-Ditchfield, alongside a telling comment that, 'we have not won anything yet but can see improvements'. After a substantial fundraising effort, the new boathouse was opened in October 2007, significantly restructured, along with two new boats.

The first name mentioned in the colours book was H.Y. Ganderton (March 1912 Senate Rowing), and he was followed by G.M. Lister. Both made a great impression on college sports. James Atkinson was another significant figure in the success of the college's boat club during the 1930s. He captained both the college and University boat clubs to many rowing triumphs.

As reported in the 1993 *College Record*, 1992 was a very strong year, perhaps helped by the college's purchase of an Ergo rowing training machine. St John's celebrated coming second on the first day of the Durham Regatta.

The opening of the refurbished boat house was held in October 2008. Although the exterior has remained largely unchanged, the entire structure has been rebuilt and allows for greater storage space.

Richard Morton (boat club captain 2008–9) writes:'St John's College boat club is in a strong position to go into the college's centenary year. The recent growth of competitive rowing at John's (for which much credit must go to the previous senior tutor, Stephen Hampton) has given us our largest squad in recent memory, with two competitive VIIIs in both the men's and women's squads. In 2008 for the first time ever we sent two men's VIIIs to the Head of the River Race in London, with the 1st VIII finishing 256th – higher than ever before, to our knowledge. Our women's squad is stronger than ever, and we hope to send a crew to the women's Head for the first time next year. With a series of regatta victories at the start of the 2008 season and a lot of strength in depth, we are confident of building on last year's VIII's victory at the Durham Regatta. Perhaps the greatest strength of the boat club is that almost all of our rowers have started as novices here at John's. Our novice crews have been very competitive recently, winning the women's Novice Cup in 2007, and every member of the 1st VIII at the Tideway in 2008 learned to row in our Novice Cup crews. Widening participation clearly need not compromise success. With the recent acquisitions of a new eight (the Revd Crossley) and a generously donated new four (Sarum), as well as sponsorship from Benfield [formerly Ernst & Young] and a newly refurbished boathouse, we have one of the best fleets of any college boat club. However, even more important for our current and future success is the large number of committed, talented individuals available to us. The combination of these makes our goal of becoming the best college boat club in Durham, although ambitious, seem quite achievable.'

Croquet

St John's achieved notoriety as the college's croquet team gained an entry in the 1977 *Guinness Book of Records*. Jonathan Pye (1974–7) remembers:'Between 12 and 15 June 1976 four of us who were undergraduates at John's – myself, Andy Parkinson, Don Lancaster and Kevin Burke – broke the world record for the longest croquet match in history. We played throughout day and (floodlit) night and got into the *Guinness Book of Records* as well as raising a considerable amount of money, which was split between the college fund and Save the Children Fund. We got tremendous support from the college and had a great team of people who

Susan and Dominique

In 1997, a manifesto promise of the newly-elected services manager, Dom Black, was to name the laundry in Cruddas 'Susan' and the JCR shop 'Dominique'. The brass plaques remain, to the bemusement of current students.

St John's 1997–8 mixed basketball team.

fed us and helped us achieve what we did.' A medical team had to be on standby at all times. This world record attempt made an impression on young Mark Yates, who, when playing croquet later in the summer with his friends, was seen to lie down between shots, thinking this was the correct procedure, not realizing it was the medical advice for the 24-hour marathon. In the past decade the college has seen something of a croquet revival, the 'thwack' of the wood resounding around the Cranmer lawns.

The 1976 world record setting 24-hour croquet team: Jonathan Pye, Andy Parkinson, Don Lancaster, Kevin Burke.

Johnian Romances

St John's has acted as unwitting matchmaker for innumerable couples within its walls and environs. Perhaps it's the 'romance' of the Bailey, the cathedral and riverside settings, no shortage of picturesque walks on a lazy Sunday afternoon, or just the simple fact that many students hope to meet the 'love of their life' in the intense years of their undergraduate studies. The Christian underpinning of St John's has led to the higher than average proportion of marriages between Johnians (since 1966 when Cranmer Hall 'went mixed').

Before this: 'There was, of course, a little contact between the men's college and the women's (St Mary's and St Hild's). One or two romances flourished, but the women's colleges maintained a strict discipline of a kind that today would be described as "Victorian". It might be added that many of the men were already engaged or had someone in the background at home. Married students were almost unknown … it was taken for granted that marriage would normally wait until a man had gone down from the university' (H. Wilkinson, 1920–5). John Oliver remembers: 'One of the great things about Durham in the early 1950s was the age differential between the sexes. Being ex-servicemen the males were two or three years older than the women, who are more mature than their same-age male counterparts. And it was possible to have real friendships across the divide free of romantic entanglement – although many Johnians did meet their future wife there.'

Hazel Harrison, wife of chaplain Peter, remembers: 'Babysitters [for staff children] were no problem, there was always

Timothy and Mally Yates, married in St Mary-the-Less in December 1968; the Yates at college reunion, 2005.

Ronald Williams with Desmond and Dorothy Treanor outside St Mary-the-Less in 1954.

a ready supply of men and their girlfriends happy for extra time together to hold hands.'

Of course, the number of Johnians who have met their significant other at St John's (or in the wider Durham environs) is almost impossible to quantify, but here are a few stories of college romances and weddings held in the college chapel.

John Rogan (1946–9 and 1952–4) recalls: 'When Dougie Michell [chaplain] got engaged to Miss Whewell, a tutor, we thought it only right to bring them together, so we went down and brought all her furniture into his flat. Good naturedly, he asked that it might be returned. Instead we took his furniture down to her flat along with her own.'

Bishop Ronald Williams married Desmond and Dorothy Treanor at St Mary-the-Less. Desmond remembers: 'After five happy years at St John's I married Dorothy Forster, who had been the principal's secretary for eight years, in the college chapel on 8th July 1954. We were the first couple to 'pledge their troth' in St Mary-the-Less 'within living memory'. The reception was held in the College Hall and gardens, but nothing stronger than a fruit cup was allowed as all alcohol was forbidden in those days!'

Jeremy and Daphne Hutchinson, were married in the chapel on 31 July 1956, 'halfway through my Diploma of Theology studies. We were very blessed, being allowed to get married so soon. We had met in Oxford three years before in 1953. When we told the Bishop of Stepney (where I intended to work) about our engagement, he said that the rule was, "No marriage within a

year of becoming a deacon or being ordained priest." So we thought that made 1959 the earliest we could get married. But something made the bishop come up with another idea. The rule would still be kept if we married a year before I became a deacon! The college very kindly agreed with his suggestion, and arranged for us to live in the top floor of Canon H.E.W. Turner's house in number 13 The College. St John's gave us a wonderful start to married life, on the whole. Wives weren't entirely thought of as a good thing. The only worship in college Daphne was allowed to come to with me (apart from our wedding service) was evening prayer on Saturdays. But in those days the only college chapel was St Mary-the-Less, and it might have been a bit of a squash if all the wives were allowed in.

'We came back just before our golden wedding and marvelled at the refurbishment of St Mary's. The only scruffy thing in the whole place was the box for the hymn-board numbers I had made 50 years before. I hurried home and made a new one in oak.'

Mally Yates (née Shaw) remembers: 'I met my future husband [Tim] on the day I came to be interviewed as tutor for women in 1966. We were married in St Mary-the-Less just before Christmas 1968; the first wedding resulting from the 'Cranmer experiment'. John Cockerton conducted the service, and Jim Hickinbotham preached. The week before the wedding I went down to the police station to warn them that there would be a lot of extra cars that day and watched with amusement as the PC write in his notebook that it was to be at "St Mary-the-Lass"!'

It is not just students who meet their match while at St John's. There have also been a number of notable staff pairings. Like Principal Wallis, John Cockerton was unmarried when he arrived in Durham, but he surprised the whole college in June 1974 by announcing his engagement to Diana Smith, a student at Cranmer Hall. They married in Nether Poppleton, York, that August. Warden Timothy Yates remembers: 'The Cranmer body was so stunned by this [news] that for a long time they seemed unable to come into the common room for coffee!' With a note of unplanned humour, the hymn announced at the following morning's chapel service (in the new undergraduate chapel) was 'God Moves in Mysterious Ways, His Wonders to Perform'.

Margaret Masson writes: 'College has always been a fertile ground for romance. Dozens, maybe hundreds over the years! I also know about college romances from personal experience! I got to know Robert Song, now my husband, when I came back to John's as senior tutor. We had met briefly the previous year when I was passing through Durham with a group of American students on a British Isles study tour. I knocked on Michael Vasey's door, but he was out so I tried the next door along to ask for paper and pencil to leave a note. Inside was the new young ethics tutor, Robert Song. Little did I know (although Robert claims to have had an intimation!). It took us a while (and no little help from Michael Vasey, who at a couple of crucial moments acted as go-between) to decide to pursue the romance option.'

Amabel Craig remembers: 'Thanks to fellow "theolog", Rachel Bird, I was persuaded to ask a tall, dark and handsome man from St Antony's Priory, Claypath to the 1997 Bailey Ball. (Although known as my "random monk" he was not preparing for the habit!) Unexpectedly, cupid's arrow struck that night and almost two years later, at the top of the cathedral's tower with ring and champagne, Jim proposed. We married just as Jim started his training at Cranmer Hall in September 1999.'

Johnian romances continue and generations of 'Johnian children' are born.

The Arts

What St John's may have sometimes lacked on the sports field has been more than made up for the variety of artistic endeavour in the arts. Principal David Day appreciated this in the mid-1990s: 'In the Arts John's may be said to excel … All in all, the range of talent is breathtaking'

College Record, 1994–5

MUSIC

Alumni remember a skiffle group in the 1960s, although sadly no photograph of the group has come to light. (In those days, no one would have thought of taking a photo.) Julia Tolley, an honorary member of college, remembers that the play list included 'Careless Love', 'Rock My Soul' and 'Wabash Cannonball'.

Another musical group was Ebenezer, a 'Christian rock group', which played gigs between 1971 and 1973 around Durham and the surrounding villages, for youth groups and in Newcastle Civic Centre. It even toured schools in Dorset. The members were Paul Medlock, Derek Little, Andrew Wells and

Georgina Wilczek (née Luck) remembers the choral group Camerata: 'In 1998, under my leadership, a smaller group of 10 to 12 singers from the choir called St John's Camerata formed to perform a mixture of unaccompanied sacred and secular music at various college events. Our inaugural event was performing Faure's Cantique de Jean Racine *at the college's Development Dinner at Auckland Castle. We also performed throughout Durham, regular college Music Society concerts, even singing folksongs on the river in the summer. In 1999, we received college funding to make a cd, recorded over two days in Hild/Bede chapel. It sold 500 copies. Many members of this original group continue to meet to this day. In 1999, members of St John's Orchestra's brass section joined up with St John's Camerata to perform an impressively loud rendition of Rutter's* Gloria *under Jemima Peterken.'*

Chris Edmondson, who was organ scholar and who enjoyed combining the two varying styles of music: 'I think there is richness in variety as far as music in worship is concerned.'

Other bands have waxed and waned through the years, the gathering of like-minded students with spare time into the early hours have led to any number of musical groupings, with varying degrees of success. A part-Johnian Christian contemporary band, Coastal Dune, achieved considerable success throughout the university and on the Christian music scene between 1998 and 2000. Johnians Becky Drake (née Harding), Andy Wolfe and Jonathan Heasley were joined by Chad's men Nick Drake, Stephen Dawson and Nick Thorley to write and perform their unique, Christian-based music, and they made three CDs/EPs at the Crossgate Centre recording studio.

The DJ 'outfit' Daylight Robbery began in the 1980s and continues to provide a variety of music for social events at St John's and other colleges. It is described in a 1997 yearbook as having 'moved on from Spanish disco hits to the dance experience as it is now'.

From the college Concert Society in 1973 to the college orchestra and the Wallis Organ Scholarship, adequate support and recognition has been given to the appreciation, creation and development of a range of classical music. The college orchestra has enjoyed a good reputation. A report in the 1994 *College Record* appreciated the presence of another Welsh harpist, Ceri Ann Huws,

Singing Rutter's Requiem, *December 1996.*

May Day Madrigals

An important feature of choir-singing in the late 90s was early morning May Day Madrigals. At just after 6am on May Day morning, a group of around 30 choir members dressed in gowns process noiselessly up and down the corridors of college, to suddenly blast out madrigals for a solid hour and a half before breakfast in Haughton. Favourite madrigals included 'Now Is The Month Of Maying', 'Tanzen und Springen' and the rather ridiculous 'Strike It Up Tabor'.

Preparing the music outside the Crossgate Centre, St Margaret's Garth at 6.30am (left). From 1997 to 1999, the tradition became so popular that the choir even met up at St Margaret's Garth to catch the second year livers-out first, and returning throughout College; no corner was safe! Also traditional was the rapid pursuit by students with mugs and saucepans full of water, and an army of water guns; we would often end up singing on the run! In 1997 the 30-strong choir even ended up on Cranmer roof, much to the astonishment of the college officers wondering where the music was coming from on their way out of chapel!

Georgina Wilczek

and a Christmas concert included the overture to Mozart's *Magic Flute*, movements from Grieg's *Peer Gynt Suite* and 'When I'm Sixty-four'. The choir was also planning to perform Fauré's *Requiem* alongside the orchestra. The orchestra was the largest college one in the university. It was popular and friendly, operating an open-door policy, an 'excellent sound and some fantastic termly orchestra socials' (Georgina Wilczek). Through the years, the university orchestra has enjoyed a strong Johnian presence, particularly three out of the four years when the college provided the leader of the symphony orchestra and many of the cellists – indeed, it was known in college as 'the college orchestra, with reinforcements' (*College Record, 2006*).

'The main highlight of 1995's autumn term was a joint orchestra–choir performance of Britten's *St Nicholas Cantata* in St Nic's Church in the

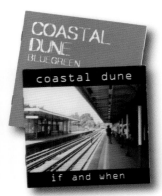

The John's-Chad's band, Coastal Dune, enjoyed considerable success between 1998–2000, recording three cds (in the Cross Gate Centre), a single for National Marriage Week 2000 and appearance in an article in the Guardian.

marketplace. This was a tremendously popular event, including Tim McVittie heading the soprano semi-chorus from the balcony because many sopranos were ill. He had a fantastic falsetto because he sang as an alto with the cathedral choir, and he sent the finest top Cs ringing out at such a volume that no one could quite believe it! There were many really good singers in the college at the time, including Claire Bessent, Nick Warden, Katrina Murray, James Roscoe, Tim McVittie and Ruth Spencer. In the autumn of 1995 several of this group put on a Durham University Music Society concert full of barbershop favourites, such as "Frankie and Johnny" and "A Nightingale Sang in Berkeley Square".

Throughout the late 1990s Anne Harrison, the college's music coordinator, was a tremendous support and always used to make sure that St John's various music groups were fairly represented in the end-of-term cathedral services.

Jenny Hill, who studied music at John's from 1995 to 1998, was a fantastic harpist and could often be seen wheeling the concert instrument with great difficulty over the Bailey cobbles backwards and forwards between music venues. One of her most requested solos was Hasselman's *La Source*, which she performed effortlessly. She also adapted Mozart's Flute and Harp Concerto to give an outstanding performance in Leech Hall with oboist Helen Lofthouse.

In 1999 Helen Dayananda packed out the Music Department's concert hall with a memorable solo performance of Pergolesi's *Stabat Mater* with soprano Emma Peaurt. Nick Wray (1995–8) was a fantastic jazz singer and could often be heard performing around college. He sounded very like a young Frank Sinatra, and it was great to listen to him.'

The choir has continued to develop, performing challenging and unusual pieces. At the visit of John Sentamu, the Archbishop of York, and college visitor in 2006, the college chapel choir sang a Duke Ellington anthem. The number of choral scholarships has increased dramatically in recent years. In 1996 the choir led worship in Gibside Chapel, candlelit choral evensong on the Bowes Estate and choral evensongs in Wakefield Cathedral, High House Methodist Chapel, Upper Weardale, culminating in a tour in July 2006. Further engagements included Westminster Abbey, St Martin-in-the-Fields and the Chapel Royal of St Peter-ad-Vincula.

THEATRE

The opening of Leech Hall in 1987 allowed for greater space for dramatic productions. Al Muir (1985–8) remembers: 'I have the honour of having directed the first theatre performance in the (then) new Leech Hall, *Blood and Ice* – a play about the life and imagination of Mary Shelley by Liz Lochead. I'd taken the decision to direct the play in the round, so John Rudin had meticulously hired the technical equipment so we could achieve a professional standard of lighting for such a theatre. Period costumes had been sourced, thanks to Caroline Sanderson's and Pippa Alderson's resourceful and determined efforts. To maximize our audience we'd also managed to persuade a professional photographer to take photos for posters and the programme.

'Over supper one evening David Pain, JCR president, mentioned that Principal Etchells was having second thoughts about the project, the key issue being that our production would be performed only days before the official opening of Leech Hall by the Queen Mother. I met with Ruth so I could remind her how long ago she had agreed to our booking the hall. (I recall my concern when making the booking was that the hall would not be complete for our performances, but relaxed when it became apparent that a date had been fixed for HRH to open it!) Ruth's concerns about the damage we might inflict on the pristine hall were something none of us had anticipated. She was charming and firm. We explored all diplomatic avenues and came to the point where Ruth said she had never previously broken her word to a student and wasn't going to start now, provided that I could assure her that Leech Hall would be left without blemish for the official opening. I did, it was and thereby hangs a tale for those who doubt the sincerity of college principals, students or indeed thespians. As *Palatinate* reported, "*Blood and Ice* heralds the

The first dramatic performance in Leech Hall.

opening of the new Leech Hall in John's … the mood of this modern play well suited to the adaptable new venue, which is a welcome addition to Durham's theatrical scene".'

It was not just John's Hall students who showed artistic flair. Nick Seward (Cranmer Hall 1995–8) remembers: 'The Sapphire Theatre Company was an independent student drama society within St John's college, formed in December 1994 by Marcus Ramshaw and Nicholas Seward with the express aim of fostering better relationships between the students of Cranmer Hall and John's Hall and of promoting drama in general. The company began in ambitious style, with a lavish production of Shakespeare's *Much Ado About Nothing*, selling out all three nights it was performed. It was staged with a 1920s setting with a new musical score composed by Andrew Green and performed by the "Clever Young Things", Emmie Clines and Mark Mallabone. Since then the company has staged two further productions: *An Inspector Calls* and a medieval *Romeo and Juliet* in full period costume' (*College Record*, 1996).

The Bailey Theatre Company is one of St John's long-lived (in student memories at least) artistic institutions. One such example is the 1998 production of *Amadeus* with full-period costumes loaned from Bowes Museum. In 2007, it staged six productions, including a new translation of *Antigone* staged in the chapel and the Summer Shakespeare, bringing successes in the University's annual D'Oscar awards. Success continued into 2008 with a production of *Dr Faustus* also performed in the chapel winning best play award at that year's D'Oscars.

Lois Stuckenbruck remembers: 'On 25 November [1995] St John's College gave a performance that stands as a testimony to the teamwork and dedication found within the college. *Up and Down the City Walls, In and Out the Bailey* was the exuberant title given to the collage of pantomime, music and dance, which for a brief two hours revived some of the Bailey's past residents. Its inspiration was derived from David Day's archival excavations and a matching venue [the cathedral] to drool over … There were at least 30 producers and four script editors/writers. The conflicting schedules of the over 100 cast members meant that each piece would need to be rehearsed individually, requiring no fewer than eight directors [and two stage managers, Chris Taylor and Kate West]. What emerged was an enchanting evening for the appreciative audience of nearly 400. They will not soon forget listening and watching Fauré's *Pavane* rise like incense through the ancient towers. Nor will Luke Walton's delicious reading of the politically correct version of Noah and the 'Above Average

Watching a Summer Shakespeare performance on the library lawn.

Deposition of Atmospheric Moisture' be memory unallocated for future reference. Certainly the bagpipes will have awakened a few of the Scottish prisoners from their sleep-enhanced state! The most frequent response was "What an enormous amount of talent in such a small college!"' (*College Record*, 1996). About £1,700 was raised for the Development Campaign.

The college has, inevitably put on a number of Shakespearean plays. Richard Horton (1983–6) writes of 'a thoroughly memorable performance of *Much Ado About Nothing* in the richly atmospheric location of my favourite riverside corner, madrigals on the river'. The year 1996 saw a pantomime version of *Romeo & Juliet*. 'The abiding memory is that of the bursar [Robert Scott-Biggs] bestriding the two halls like a pocket-colossus and giving a mellow and indulgent audience ten minutes of free-range improvisation' (Day, *College Record*, 1997). In 2006 the second post-examination Shakespeare, *Much Ado About Nothing*, was performed: 'Once again it strikes me as very extraordinary not merely than an entire play should be cast, rehearsed and performed in five days, but that it should be performed once, on the Cranmer lawn, and be open to anyone, free of charge' (Sykes, *College Record*, 2006).

'I am not sure if St John's has ever before been able to claim even a part share in a novelist. We await publication of Cathy Wilcox's first novel [published as Catherine Fox], *Angels and Men*, early in the New Year [1997]. The book has nothing to do with St John's but just happens to be set in a university college containing a theological hall in a north of England cathedral city' (Day, *College Record*, 1996).

'*In faith is our victory' speaks to me of the imagination of faith – the kind of imaginative, creative exploration of Christian identity that was/is the hallmark of St John's and also the kind of steadfast loyalty – to God, to the college, to each other, that I have seen in so many of its members.*

Margaret Masson, senior tutor 1992–9

Food, Glorious Food!

If, like an army, a body of students works on its stomach, it is remarkable that St John's has survived! The college has always been able to provide three meals a day, despite numerous food shortages throughout the war years, and during the particularly fierce winter of 1979 when the Bailey was virtually under siege from heavy snowfall. Meals are served in Haughton dining room, although ordinands began to separate themselves in the mid-1950s, with Bowes dining room used as the Cranmer dining room from 1958.

During the college's first 50 years evening meals were served formally. James Atkinson remembers that in the 1930s the butler, Dennison, wore tails for the evening meals, while students wore white collars, black ties and black coats, with gowns over it all. The Senior Man would say grace in Latin before the meal and the chaplain would close the meal formally. Students were given a place in the dining room for the whole term. George Parkinson remembers: 'The butler and staff served the students at mealtimes in the 1940s, which were very formal, although a John's blazer was an "acceptable" alternative at lunchtime. Duty rotas

were introduced as numbers grew, as it soon became unmanageable for Dennison and Harry to wait on everyone each mealtime. Tables were covered for every meal with white linen table cloths, at the insistence of Principal Wallis. He deemed it to be representative of respectable dining, as gentlemen should. Williams did away with this formality shortly after his arrival, creating a more relaxed approach to mealtimes in college. Having said that, gowns still had to be worn and the formalities of Latin grace were still carried out at the commencement of each meal.'

Rationing remained in force until 1953, and students gave their rationing book to the housekeeper but kept some coupons back for provisions for afternoon tea. Despite the formality, the food was of a much lower quality than today, largely because of the inevitable food shortages in post-war Britain and rapidly increasing numbers of students. H. Wilkinson

ST. JOHN'S COLLEGE
FESTIVAL DINNER

Wednesday, 26th May, 1954

The 1967–8 food book makes for a fascinating read…

(1920–25) remembers:'Economy was in the air and our food while adequate was by no means exciting – porridge for breakfast with now and then some egg "substitute". Cheese for lunch. Dinner, the main meal, soup, meat and vegetables, and a rather stodgy pudding. It was all done with great dignity. The students in dark suits and gowns assembled, each table served by a waiter. Then the butler opened the staff door, and in they came. Then the Latin grace was said by the Senior Man and I can still remember it.'

George Parkinson, a student in the 1940s, remembers:'Eggs were severely rationed during wartime. I can recall being allowed only one or two each term, and it was quite a celebration when they arrived. Woe betide it if any were discovered to be "off".' Parkinson recalls on more than one occasion hearing the shout 'Dennison, this egg is rotten!' The affronted student would be guaranteed to cause a bit of a scene in his anxiety to obtain a fresh one.

G.P. Wedgewood (1948–52) remembers:'In those days we operated an informal care system for those stricken with minor problems such as colds. We could absent ourselves from breakfast, but a friend could request a pot of tea and toast to bring down from the kitchen, leaving the recipient's name with the kitchen staff. One morning my friend, Bert Steed, asked me to do this for him. I followed the procedure and was sitting in Bert's room when a knock at the door revealed both Principal Williams and

Latin Grace

Martin Stevens (1955–60) remembers the grace as: 'Benedice, Domine, huic ibo in usum nostrum, nobisque in servitutam tuam, per Jesum Christum Dominum Nostrum. Amen. (Bless, O Lord, these gifts to our use and us in your service, through Jesus Christ our Lord. Amen.).

An item in the 1967–8 JCR food book requests a translation of the end-of-meal grace, followed by the suggestion: 'I'm blest if I'm going to eat this blessed food.'

the domestic bursar. The principal said "What's all this, Mr Steed?" More fussily the domestic bursar asked, "What's the matter, Mr Steed?" To which, quick as a flash, Bert said "Malnutrition, woman!" It was in the days of food rationing and probably Bert was not alone in his evaluation.'

The situation didn't improve in the 1950s. Tom Thompson (1956–60) remembers:'There was a small demonstration within the college in 1957–8 in respect of the food served in the dining hall. It left much to be desired, especially the breakfast menu, at which bacon rolls played a large part! They were usually burned on the outside and stone cold on the inside. A small deputation carried a bacon roll on a silver salver with some ceremony up to high table and placed it in front of the principal. The food improved immediately – and we never again received bacon rolls!'

The following extracts are from the food book of the JCR food committee between October 1967 and June 1968, which was dedicated:'To Matron – with Love!'

'I think the kitchen staff must have got the sequence of the courses muddled today – and missed one out. Melon – usually provided before the main course – has about as much nutritious content as a "smartie".'

'When will matron realize that in her efforts to economize – viz. the mass purchase of kidneys for breakfast – she is in fact wasting a great deal of money, for a more revolting prospect than kidneys at 8.20 am (with the possible exception of matron at 8.20 am) I can hardly imagine. I hate kidneys!'

'The chef may want his shorn locks preserved for posterity, but does he have to preserve them in my jelly?'

'I appreciate the need for tinned food, but must some of us be inflicted with eating the tin as well?'

And so on for the whole year. A few positive comments were noted:

'What an excellent meal tonight! No "BUTs". The first course was well cooked, including the sprouts. Melon is always a welcome fresh fruit as a second course, best eaten without sugar.'

Left: The smiling faces of the serving staff c.2000.

Above: Haughton dining room c.1936.

Inset: Menu for 1953 festival dinner.

Above: 'Max the caterer, a long-suffering marvellous man who struggled with no money with which to cook us the food.' Adrian Beney 1983–6.

Left: The new canteen-style serving hatch in the 1970s.

'The grapefruit was very welcome.'

And so rationing stopped, but the food didn't improve. Robert Wright (1966–70) remembers: 'The food was truly awful in the 1960s. Matron was in charge and looked out for job lots of cheap food she could buy to keep costs down. A year's supply of "kidneys in jelly" was the last straw for many of us and propelled us to acquire girlfriends in the newer colleges where the food was better.' I think it was kidneys in jelly we buried. I don't know the number of the room but it was in Linton wing. I didn't know much about the sacraments in those days, being a mere lawyer, but I am sure burying the food was a visible sign of something we felt deeply. Mind you, coming back in the early hours meant creeping through the kitchen, and I remember crunching the cockroaches under foot.'

Charlotte South (née Owen, 1973–6) summarizes food in the 1970s: 'Food has often been a topic of conversation in St John's. The Sunday morning smell, a combination of eggs for breakfast boiled to death alongside the Sunday cabbage, which seemed to go on at the same time in the morning! The pink/green puddings, the horribly over-salted soup, Saturday and Sunday tea at 5.15 –

Regulations from the 1920s

'Gowns must be worn at all meals (except lunch). Those who wish to be absent from meals should give their names (as long as possible beforehand) to the butler. A dark coat (black or navy blue) with a stiff collar and black tie must be worn for dinner. Plus fours are not allowed at dinner time.'

chips on Saturday, salad on Sunday, chicken fricassee (it had other names!). It always seemed that the other colleges fed their students better than ours did, but I don't know if that was really the case.'

Adrian Beney (1983–6) remembers the famous 'chicken grace':

'For chicken hot, for chicken cold
For chicken new, for chicken old
For chicken roast, for chicken stuffed,
We thank you Lord, we've had enough.'

Adrian Vincent (1990–3) remembers that into the 1990s 'food was pretty dire, worse than in any other college. At the start of term you were given a meals pass, which stated whether you were a meat eater or a vegetarian. No choice was provided at

Table at 2007 Christmas formal in Leech Hall.

Above: Kitchen staff preparing for John's Day.
Left: No longer 'dire'! A dessert, 2007.

meals – just a meat option and a vegetarian option. If you didn't like the meat option that day you were not allowed to have the vegetarian meal because your pass did not permit it. Bread and butter were, however, provided, so you had the dilemma of another meal consisting of toast or to increase the student debt still further with a trip to Pizzaland.'

In the 21st century the food has improved and is rated among the best in the university in student satisfaction surveys. Alison Bradshaw took over as in-house catering manager in 1991 in the newly refurbished kitchens. By 2002 she had a newly trained, skilled team of Lorraine, head chef, and John, the sous chef. The Bailey Ball is one of the hardest days for staff, providing meals simultaneously for 150 guests in Leech Hall and 80–100 in

Haughton dining room. The Bowes dining room is used for food preparation. Staff work from 7 am until after 10 pm. As a result, Saturday 'brunch' is served an hour later than usual the next day. In the past, students have helped serve meals, but have been known to get too distracted! As balls are themed, the menu is too, aiming for the 'wow factor'. Other occasions also merit themed menus, including Valentine's Day and St Patrick's Day. Alison Bradshaw comments that students' demands have changed over the years, as they travel more before coming to university, and requirements for special diets increase through cultural needs and food intolerances.

In the 1990s formal meals were held each Sunday until the JCR passed a motion to hold only a few each term. Stephen Hampton (senior tutor 2004–7) reinstated them to once a fortnight, and they are now held once a week. An 'early tea' is provided in Bowes before the formal meal.

All beverages provided in college are fairly traded, and the college has 'fair trade status'.

> "John's in three words: simply the best!"
> Ian Andrew, tutor 1994–2005

High Days and Holy Days

In one respect college life is full of 'high days', enlivening the routine of termly life, celebrating the rhythm of academic life and reminding the 'student bubble' of a wider frame of reference in the university's and college's history. The 2009 centenary is planned to be a great celebration, commemorating and celebrating those who have lived and worked in St John's College.

What follows is a selection of significant events in college life, royal visits, anniversaries and regular, termly events. Of course, it could easily have been a fully illustrated section. Undoubtedly, most students have a large selection of photographs of groups of friends in formal and fancy dress and having fun. This is of limited interest to a wider audience (and the editor has not received many such photographs), so more formal events and photographs have been chosen.

After the first day of term in 1909, the first major 'high day' was the opening ceremony for Cruddas House on 14 March 1913. Unfortunately, William Cruddas died in 1912, so he was represented at the ceremony by Miss Eleanor Cruddas and her sister, Miss Florence Cruddas (see photograph on p.14). Their elder sister, Dora, was indisposed on the day. Nevertheless, Dora Cruddas remained the college's most significant benefactor from

this time until her death in 1929. It was described as 'in the nature of a family gathering [of] those more especially in sympathy with the main purpose of the institution' (*Durham Johnian*, 1930). A preliminary service was held in the morning in the college chapel, with Charles Wallis, then vice-principal, playing the organ. Invited guests included the Bishop of Newcastle, the Bishop of Jarrow, Bishop Tucker, the Dean of Canterbury (president of council), the Revd J.E. Watts-Ditchfield (council chairman) and Principal Dawson-Walker. Other guests included professors and canons and a variety of vicars from the area, 'including a large contingent of

Right: Distinguished guests at 1958 Jubilee lunch, including: Dr Sam Watson; Bishop of Durham; Dr M.H. Harland; Dean of Bristol, Very Revd D.E.W. Harrison; The Earl of Scarborough, Chancellor of Durham University; The Principal; Archbishop of York, Dr A.M. Ramsey; Mrs Ramsey; Bishop of Leicester, Rt Revd R.R. Williams; Mayor of Durham, Vice-Chancellor, Sir James Duff; Mrs Wild; Dean of Durham, Dr J.H.S. Wild; Mrs Harland and the Mayoress Miss H. Duff.

Above: The visit of Her Majesty the Queen to Durham in 1951. Contemporaries remember that as the royal cortège drove along the Bailey, Johnsmen stood on Haughton steps and mothers and children waved from the door of Number 5 South Bailey.

ladies'. (The Bishop of Durham was out of the country.) The address text was Matthew 27:51, with the theme of 'the only work which will endure was that which was based on self-sacrifice'.

The Bishop of Chelmsford, J.E. Watts-Ditchfield, addressed the congregation as Miss Eleanor Cruddas 'opened' the house with a silver-gilt key, 'the house which will be dedicated to the name of Mr Cruddas for ever'. The architect, Mr Potts, who was also present, 'received warm congratulations upon the effectiveness of the design and the excellence with which it has been carried out'. A luncheon was held in the dining room, and it was a day enjoyed by all who attended.

In 1930 St John's College 'came of age', celebrating the 21st anniversary of its foundation. A series of celebrations was planned, a reunion party and, slightly later, a replacement east window for the chapel in memory of Dora Cruddas, in addition to a celebration of the college's 'birthday'.

In 1953 Principal Williams was appointed to the bishopric of Leicester. His wife, Cecily, remembers: 'The college concert was the best ever and was based almost entirely on Ronald's elevation to the episcopate ... There was an enormous party for Johnians past and present, at which Ronald was presented with his cross and ring; the cross a replica of that which he had had designed for the college chapel altar ... Matron surpassed herself with the Christmas dinner; it was the greatest feast the college had enjoyed, and we all did full justice to it. At the end of the meal the Senior Man, Neil Robinson, in a brilliant little speech, presented me with a gift from all the men: the Everest book and a really wonderful steam iron. The domestic staff of the college had a tea party for us and gave us a tea service that we have since used for every important occasion at bishop's lodge.' Around 35 students managed the long journey south to 'The Prin's' consecration and, later, enthronement.

George Parkinson (1944–8), recollects: 'The only day I can recall the doors not being locked at a fixed time, was VE Day. College door rules were disbanded for that evening – as was the rule on alcohol consumption, as far as I can remember!'

Left: A student rag in the Market Place from the late-1940s

quickly stopped), and dyed milk – if one received dyed milk at breakfast one had to have a (spurious) exam.

The college's social calendar now consists of one ball a term (the Bailey Ball as the highlight), five formal dinners and John's Day. The college's festival dinners are held once a term: Christmas, Ascension tide, and in the summer. They are an occasion for a formal dinner and, in former decades, formal toasts. Gowns are still required attire, and the food is of the highest quality.

JOHN'S DAY

The highlight of the Johnian calendar is John's Day. Held in mid-June, after exams, this is a full day of events, food and silliness.

Term-time constraints mean that the event is not held as the college's feast day (the feast of St John the Evangelist is 26 December) but as a celebration of college life. Under Stephen Sykes the celebration was tied in with the festival of St John before the Latin Gate on 6 May. One highlight through the years is the raft race from one side of the Wear to the other. Teams have to build their rafts, and the one that survives and reaches the other side first wins. Apart from the raft race, other events include barbecue lunch and dinner, jelly and water fights (not always together), 'bouncy tents', pie-eating and the annual college awards.

Margaret Masson (senior tutor 1992–9) remembers John's Day as 'an annual highlight, and my favourite memory of those was being on the winning (all-female) crew of the raft race one year. Jane Grieve must take most of the credit for a floatable raft: it was a glorious day, so good that we spent quite a while just splashing about in the river afterwards.'

Helen Bartlett (tutor from 1996) also remembers 'infamous John's raft races, sinking in the dirty water, if only we could've walked on it! Even Bishop Sykes sank!'

COLLEGE BALLS

'The Bailey Ball in November is our most dazzling affair,' writes Tom Pember-Finn (social chair 2007–8). 'It is held in college, and is a night of extravagance, music and high-class celebrations. The Epiphany Ball is traditionally held in a venue outside college and pays tribute to the sporting achievements of our members, while the summer ball takes place in the gorgeous

Principal Etchells' masterly exposition of the role of the Good Fairy (a developed classic); staff pantomime, December 1982.

The opening of Cranmer Hall in 1958 was timed to correspond with the college's jubilee in 1959 – 50 years of St John's College were celebrated on 23 June 1959, with the boosting of the college's development appeal and promotion of the college. A reunion was held, along with a luncheon in the college hall, 'which had undergone a rapid transformation, efficiently carried out by the domestic staff. It was a very happy and friendly occasion.' It was followed by speeches, prayers and a visit to the building site for the laying of a foundation stone: 'The sun shone, and there was a good crowd of Johnians past and present, together with members of the staff of the university and other friends of the college' (*Durham Johnian*, 1959).

An annual tradition grew up of Mischief Night around 4 November. Memories abound about pranks and jokes, which were endured by both students and staff. Former members of the domestic staff from the 1980s remember clingfilm over toilet seats, lightbulbs planted in the gardens, pennies in the lights, which blew the fuses throughout college (a prank that was

The serious business of John's Day 2008.

Lumley Castle and is a glamorous evening (primarily for our sadly departing members) in an idyllic setting. Social events at John's are famously some of the best in Durham. They are an opportunity for the whole college to come together as a community and to participate in activities ranging from sophisticated banquets to swimming across the Wear and back. The origin of St John's social highlight, the Bailey Ball, is uncertain. The JCR minutes of 1974 mention a formal ball held in early November, although it is not named. A double ticket cost £5 and included 'a very good meal, a folk-artist, a rock group, a formal dance band, a disco, and a special attraction'. Remuneration was given to those who offered help during the ball. It was held in Haughton dining room, the only room large enough to host so many students. Margaret Masson remembers the Bailey Ball as 'a wonderful event, and the way the whole main part of college was transformed overnight was magical. I think my all-time favourite was the *Lord of the Rings* theme. I also remember Jo Brand – just before she became really famous – as the comedian one year.'

CHRISTMAS PANTOMIMES AND REVUES

Margaret Masson remembers: 'The annual pantomimes were hugely enjoyable and (we thought) very funny – not always intentionally so! The staff pantomime had been one item in a more general college review when I started as a resident tutor in 1983. When I returned as senior tutor in 1992 they had died a death. I reinstated them and had great fun reinventing "the tradition": I insisted that the principal had to take the role of fairy godmother (as Ruth Etchells had frequently done a decade earlier, see photo on opposite page), putting everything to rights in the end. This role, of course, called for appropriate female attire and definitely tights! David Day gamely responded and was a wonderful pantomime Dame through the years, adding his own layers of expectation and tradition. I still have the silver size 9 sparkling court shoes I found to encourage him in his first appearance. Some great memories of John Pritchard as (I think) Cinderella. And also, my nine-month-old daughter, Iona's pantomime debut as (can this be right?) a rugby ball doubling up as the new principal of St John's.'

> *The message of 'Welcome Home' on the banners you see on Freshers' Sunday each year really are true. How, in a few words, would you sum up the spirit of St John's? Like Nowhere Else.*
>
> Phil Thomas 2002–6

The Johnian Family

St John's College has a reputation for being the friendliest college in Durham, probably owing to a combination of its small size and Christian ethos. A vital part of this strong sense of community is the 'family' of St John's: the staff, the Senior Common Room, alumni and so on. As early as 1952, the staff–student relationships were described as being like a family, a sentiment echoed today.

STAFF

The fact that many staff members remain at St John's for decades reflects what Stephen Sykes described as the 'humane' environment in which they work. Unfortunately, many staff members remain the 'unsung heroes' of college life, their stories difficult to trace in archived college documents. Without them, the college could not function.

The earliest staff body was a small core of principal, chaplain, tutors (in at least classics and biblical languages) and a medical officer. Additional tutoring was given in music and elocution, and in 1930 this was the responsibility of Gertrude M. McLeod, probably the first female member of tutorial staff. During these years, many staff members held a variety of roles, adding to the familial atmosphere. It is perhaps surprising to see the number of staff members who graduated through the ranks of undergraduate to tutor, bursar and even as high as vice-principal. Almost half of college's principals have held significant posts as staff members before their appointment as principal: Dawson-Walker, Wallis, Cockerton and Wilkinson.

Charles Wallis wrote: 'It is one of the great assets of St John's that the members of its staff have been so permanent and so loyal in their work for the college. This in itself has made for stability and continuity of policy' (*Old Johnian*, 1926). An alternative view is that, 'recycling staff is part of the college's environmental policy' (*College Record*, 1997).

The butler Dennison was assisted by Harry, and he was replaced by Mr Glendenning in 1958. (There seems to have been a college butler until 1954.) Other significant members of staff during this era included Mrs Gadd the matron–housekeeper until Easter 1957, who was replaced by Miss Dolly Smith. Other domestic staff members included Mrs Lizzie Hobson, the cook

for 30 years and Mrs Lily Robinson, housekeeper from 1974, who was awarded the BEM in the 1980 honours list.

'We regret that we had to say goodbye to Tom Gibbon, the gardener here for many years; a familiar figure with an inevitable flower in his cap every day, and his endless store of amusing yarns. Tom earned the respect of every member of the college simply because he was so very happy in his job' (Principal Hickinbotham's letter, 1958).

STORIES FROM THE LINEN STORES

Most students remember 'their' cleaners most fondly, and many become like 'second mams' to students, listening to all their problems. As one student said: 'Janet Alderson and Gloria Everett are the most important people in college. Their standard jobs are medical support, counselling, matchmaking and occasionally a bit of cleaning. They are more a part of the fabric of college than the

Right: Informal staff meeting in Leech Hall, 2006.

Opposite top: Former Housekeeper Lily Robinson awarded the British Empire Medal in 1980.

Below: Arthur Welsh, a member of the domestic staff c.1920.

buildings themselves. They are on first-name terms with the college ghost' (from an unattributed college webpage 1999). 'It is plain to me how much our students owe to the kindly tolerance, motherliness and good humour of those who see them on a daily basis in their own habitat' (Sykes, *College Record, 2000*).

Pauline Williams, who joined the staff in 1978, becoming housekeeper until 1997, 'could put the fear of God into the students' (and some staff members). Margaret Masson (former senior tutor) remembers: 'Pauline was a great character: like many others, I was slightly in awe of her, especially when she would be waiting for me at 9am in the morning to tell me of the previous night's shenanigans – and, more often than not, who the culprit was! Trying occasionally to dissuade her from instant justice was not always easy, and more than once I was hauled off to stand behind her as she banged on the offender's door. She had a heart of gold and was held in deep affection by most students – even the most stalwart offenders.'

Dennison, the College Butler (1919–54)

Henry Beckett Dennison (1887–1954) was fostered as an infant in Durham where he spent all his life. On leaving school at the age of 14, he joined the staff of the Castle as a hall-boy, where he met his future wife, Emily Pollard, a fellow servant. They married in 1908 and lived within the shadow of the cathedral for the rest of their lives. They had seven children, four sons and three daughters. After active service, he returned to the Castle in 1919 but later the same year was persuaded by Charles Wallis to join him at St John's as college butler, a position he held with distinction until his death in service 35 years later.

He was a loyal and devoted servant to the college, forming lifelong close friendships with college staff, respected and liked by all. The college inspectors noted in their 1952 report that he 'was a lifelong domestic servant such as one rarely meets now outside fiction'. He was churchwarden at St Mary-le-Bow for over a quarter of a century. When Charles Wallis was appointed to the incumbency of St Mary-le-Bow, they worked successfully together for the whole of his tenure. In the 1930s Dennison and his family moved to No. 17 South Bailey, next door to Canon Wallis, where he lived until his death.

I remember as a boy going to grandfather's house to watch the football cup final on TV; he always invited two or four students to his house who supported or came from the areas of the teams playing. He also had a close relationship with Ronald Williams, principal from 1945. He considered retirement on the announcement of Williams's appointment to the bishopric of Leicester, but was persuaded to stay and help the new principal settle in. Before Jim Hickinbotham had taken up his responsibilities Dennison died, only a few days short of his 67th birthday. He was a very devoted man who gave his life in Christian service.

Alan Denison, his grandson

Above: It is perhaps a testament to the familial feel of St John's that some staff members seem to remain in college for decades. Ted has been a member of the college's maintenance team 'boy and man' (he appears on the 1985 staff photo, p.43) and Howard 'the Bedel' Stevens (right) has welcomed countless students back into college on his evening shifts over the past 15 years. 'It's a real privilege,' he says. 'St John's is a place full of atmosphere and love.'

Below: Various members of the domestic staff, early 1990s.

'The domestic and support staff are beyond praise for their commitment to the college and the time they give to their work. Their tolerance and good humour need to be acknowledged and praised. They turn kittens into beautiful cats; puppies into (almost) house-trained dogs' (Stephen Sykes, 2008).

Worthy of particular mention from the past decade are Sue Hobson, Alan Usher and Alison Bradshaw, who, along with their teams, keep the college running throughout the year. Without them, students would not have been fed, housed or have any

bedding. Many members of the domestic staff 'adopt' students, and generations of graduates have fond memories of the friendly faces who greet them at 'unearthly' hours.

ADMINISTRATIVE STAFF

Of course, without the administrative staff principals would be unable to complete their duties, drowning under a sea of paperwork: grants would be lost, post unopened and students unprocessed through the admissions system. Significant changes were made to administrative structures and practices under Principal Etchells in the early 1980s. Previously, 'administration [could be] creaky and unreliable, and therefore our public face was not one which won respect. We had to develop a systematic form of

information retrieval (rather than student files in brown paper bags). All the members of this much-needed support and administrative network must be helped to feel themselves part of the team, and work for the love of the place; and yet be paid honest wages and be highly professional.' Etchells was ably assisted in her duties by 'the wonderful' Doris Kay and 'the equally wonderful' Doreen Ayling as her personal assistants.

Her successor, Anthony Thiselton, echoes her appreciation: 'I was blessed at St John's with two wonderful personal assistants: Doreen Ayling and Aileen Jones. Dorothy Dryden is also fondly remembered as senior tutor's secretary, succeeded by Fee Martin and Margaret Barrett. Aileen Jones's successor was Mrs Dorothy Greenwell. who has served as principal's personal assistant for three principals (so far …)'.

'I am constantly amazed that we are blessed with people of such quality in every department. Each year I comment on the support staff's loyalty and hard work. Such remarks may appear to be no more than conventional compliments. They are, in fact, entirely genuine. The work of the college would collapse without the support staff … Recognition of what the support staff contribute comes from many different quarters – from satisfied conference organizers who write in about our first-class customer care, to the five-minute ovation with which students greeted Howard ['the Bedel'] Stevens's appearance in the pantomime. The support staff are an integral part of the college and the stuff of their lives – a wedding, a family illness, a bereavement or even a brief but telling appearance in the film of *Jude the Obscure* – touches the whole community' (David Day, *College Record*, 1996).

College staff 1987.

TUTORS

An important part of the 'Durham difference' is the tutorial system. St John's has a strong reputation for having an excellent pastoral support system. A college tutor is available to students for pastoral support and to help them think about the process and outcomes of study. Tutors are of various professions and ages, but they are 'dedicated to and supportive of students' (Day, *College Record*, 1994) in their unique ways. For example, Lois Stuckenbruck introduces her tutees to American Thanksgiving. Another tutor presents her tutees with a red rose on graduating. They offer support and often a homely environment. Many will fondly remember Ian Andrew, a tutor for over 11 years. He often took tutees for Sunday lunch in Durham, even occasionally cooking for them in St Margaret's flats. Ian was often to be found cheering on John's teams at Maiden Castle, although not in the bar, at balls or on John's Day, because 'the last thing my tutees would want was a tutor old enough to be their grandfather watching them make fools of themselves'. He maintains contact with many tutees, being invited to weddings and written to for advice and references.

PETS

Pets have made many guest appearances in college life. The Williamses' golden cocker spaniel was a feature of college life for nearly eight years. Cecily Williams remembers: 'Westcott reigned supreme. He dominated the flat and the college. He was proclaimed as their mascot by the students; he attended all matches and was offered a seat with the cox in the boat. He invaded the men's rooms, chewed their slippers and devoured their biscuits; he marched into chapel waving his great floppy ears

and was escorted out again by a visiting bishop. Everyone loved him, everyone, that is, except, Canon Wallis, who held the view that a dog would be even worse than a wife in the principal's flat. Westcott, unfortunately for us, formed an adverse opinion of Charlie … He did, in fact, let us down on every possible occasion but he was the most lovable companion anyone could find and accompanied us on picnics, car trips and college hikes.'

Jane Grieve's gerbil, Hewy (named after theologian H.E.W. Turner), was a familiar face around college in 1973, even standing for Senior Man. He got as far as the hustings but no further because he wouldn't speak; instead he ran across the table, leaving a wet trail behind him … He also appeared in the 1973 college picture.

Ruth Etchells's pets were often seen in college: Mizzle the cat, Emmie a field spaniel with a 'slightly uneven temper' and Bonnie, a Welsh russet springer, who was 'a joy and delight'. The college pets were even guests at the visit of the Queen Mother. Stephen and Joy Sykes were joined on many occasions by Salome, their golden retriever, who even had a walk-on part as the Moon in *A Midsummer Night's Dream* in 2005.

College Prayer written by Principal Sykes

Bless, O Lord, the work of this College
Called by the name of the disciple whom you loved,
And grant that your light may so shine upon our way,
And your truth guide us,
That we may abide in your love for ever;
Through the same Jesus Christ, our Lord.
Amen

Senior Common Room, St. John's College, Durham.   4694

SENIOR COMMON ROOM

The Senior Common Room was established in 1972 under the guidance of tutor Ruth Wintle. The SCR refers both to a set of reception rooms and a body of people. Professor Jimmy Dunn, former SCR president, summarizes: 'The SCR consists of all senior members of the college community, including tutors and members of college council, together with ex-Johnians and friends of the college who live locally. The college provides a delightful suite of rooms for SCR use, with coffee facilities, newspapers and periodicals available. When free, the SCR can be booked by members for a private meeting or event without charge. Guest accommodation is also available to members for a very modest charge. Members can also make use of the college library. The SCR exists to provide a place and occasions when its members can meet in a relaxed setting and socially. The SCR in particular serves as a meeting place for members of the college with others involved in the life of the university and the city or region. Apart from the support that its members give to the college individually, the SCR also gives up to £1,000 each year for travel grants for students wishing to spend the following summer in service abroad.

'The termly programme usually includes:
- a formal dinner, to which members are encouraged to bring guests;
- an informal evening, with buffet dinner;
- Wednesday lunches during term in the SCR;
- the SCR book club.

Recent highlights have included the annual Burns' supper at the end of January (not to be missed) and a Fairtrade evening in February, when the recipient(s) of the previous year's SCR travel grant(s) report on their summer adventures. Occasionally a more adventurous trip is organized, such as to western Turkey (the cities to which letters in the Book of Revelation were sent) in 2004.'

The spouses and families of principals and staff have also played an important part in college life, offering support to students, a 'homely' environment and, often, babysitting opportunities.

ALUMNI RELATIONS

St John's College has always sought to keep in close contact with former members, a move spearheaded by Principal Wallis's detailed alumni correspondence. The college has a strong record of alumni publications, including the *Old Johnian* (1926–38) and the *Durham Johnian* (1947 onwards). There was a lull in communication in the 1960s and 1970s until Jane Grieve took over the alumni and development office, which went on to produce the college's Bulletin News and the annual *College Record* (CR).

Assistants in the alumni and development office have included Suzie Tooke, Fiona Bond, Lois Stuckenbruck (now development manager), Rachel Leonard, Ceri Huws, Miles Huckle, David Davies, Amabel Craig and Azra Aslam.

The Old Johnian Society was founded 1913 with the 'object of promoting the interests of St John's College of keeping Old Johnians all over the world in touch with their Alma Mater and one another'. An annual reunion was occasionally held in Durham along with smaller ones in Birmingham and Manchester. Fees were 2s 6d a year, according to a 1924 information leaflet.

St John's Society was founded in 1979 to mark the 70th anniversary of St John's foundation. *Fides*, the society's journal, was produced throughout the 1970s and 1980s. Another part of the society's work is to raise funds for college projects and bursaries for students in need. Annual London and Durham dinners are now held.

How can one begin to summarize what alumni have gone on to achieve in such as limited space? Of course, there have been many notable alumni, both in the Church and in many varied professions, and it would be invidious to highlight a few and miss out others. 'Like most of your readers, I guess that the search for notable alumni will begin with those who made the purple or similar progression. But I know that there are literally countless parishioners throughout the Church of England who would want to nominate their unsung incumbent as a notable cleric. The dedication, faithfulness, hard work, sacrifice and good common sense of Johnian parish priests is the intricate detailed back cloth against which some have been singled out' Neil Robinson (1947–54).

Alumni (Old Johnians)
1929: 290
1973: 1,500
2008: 4,600
Numbers are approximate, and, of course, increase steadily each year.

JCR notice board June 2008, reflecting the usual array of student activities and opportunities.

Social Action and Globalization

St John's College has always maintained a wider perspective than that of city, county or country. One of the college's founding principles is of training for mission, and it has strong connections with the Church Missionary Society (CMS) and the Church Pastoral Aid Society (CPAS). From the earliest days regular college prayer meetings were held with a worldwide focus, and Principal Wallis was particularly keen to emphasize Christianity's global nature. Missionary action groups were praised by inspectors in the first year of Cranmer Hall (1958).

A large proportion of John's Hall's first graduates became missionaries. Some students came to Durham to study for the licentiate in a year or on furlough to return to the mission field. By the 1930s a quarter of Old Johnians had worked overseas.

OVERSEAS MISSION

Through CMS St John's Hall was affiliated with Fourah Bay College in Sierra Leone. The 1927 *Old Johnian* gives much detail of how this connection was manifest. The Revd T.S. Johnson MA, BD, an Old Johnian recently appointed senior tutor of Fourah Bay College, was described as 'a cheery son of Africa … he will long be remembered in St John's for three things: – his infectious laugh and good nature, the number of his blankets, and his two hot-water bottles!'

Cranmer Hall's first report (1958) noted two parochial missions and the hosting of visitors from Nigeria, Armenia and Germany, among others. Similarly, the College Record of 1994 mentions Cranmer Hall members from Zaire, Hungary, Uganda, Kostroma (Russia), Japan, Sweden and South Africa. In 1996 Cranmer celebrated overseas links with Japan, Sweden, Uganda, Zaire, Russia, Hungary and South Africa.

A.E.H. Rutter recalls: 'Reading the obituary of Archbishop Benjamin Nwankiti (Cranmer Hall 1957–60), I am reminded of an incident in 1958. A group of us had just finished an essay that had to be handed in one Saturday evening, and we decided to have a bit of a party. Two of us were detained to fetch the Revd Ben Nwankiti, for he was a popular and respected member of the community. We burst into his room and, beating the body in the bed, shouted out, "Wake up Ben, we're going to have a party!" To our horror, a white face emerged from the sheets and a cultured English voice said, "I don't know who you are, but I'm the Archdeacon of the Upper Nile!" It later transpired that Ben was away for the weekend on a preaching engagement and that the

The college's 1949 mission to Monkwearmouth: the college's team of ordinands and tutors alongside Chaplain Peter Harrison's commissioning card.

Overseas Appointments

Each edition of the *Old Johnian* and *Durham Johnian* carried a list of appointments, both country and worldwide. In 1927:

- CMS missionaries – ten
- Asia – one in Persia, six in India, eight in China
- Parochial work – seven in Canada
- Other – eight in chaplaincy or teaching work overseas, including Chan Kwan Lam, Queen's College, Hong Kong

Students in 1996 on a mission to Kostroma, Durham's twin city in Russia, 200 miles north-east of Moscow, to rebuild the monastery of Chukloma with the Russian Orthodox Church.

Below: Local volunteers involved in the Sudan Hope project, part of the Edith Jackson Trust.

Bottom: A school in Rokon, Sudan, built by the Edith Jackson Trust in 2008. In front of it are the Head Engineer and Bishop Francis.

said archdeacon who was visiting the college, had been put to sleep in his room. Needless to say, we had to apologize to Principal Hickinbotham the next morning' (CR 2006).

Crammer students continue to be involved and concerned with worldwide learning, mission and development. Recent placements overseas have included St Paul's College, Kapsabet in Kenya, Nigeria, India, the United States, Australia, New Zealand, the Costa del Sol in Spain, Paris and the Canadian Arctic.

LOCAL MISSIONS

Part of ordinands' training at St John's has also involved local missions to nearby villages and towns. Principal Wallis (1919–45) was renowned for the open-air missions he organized. In October 1920 he led the university's missionary campaign in Stockton. A team of graduates and undergraduate 'campaigners' preached in churches and gave addresses to various church groups: 'Every opportunity was seized during the week to come into touch with all classes of people ... to bring home to Christian people in every parish the urgent need of the heathen world ... to show how that solution can be found alone in Christ's teaching' (University *Journal*, 1921). A similar mission was held in 1927.

Johnians have also been closely involved with the provision of summer camps and outings for local residents without Church connections, including supplementary Church work and parochial missions. Such laudable aims clearly demonstrate St John's evangelical Anglicanism.

Neil Robinson (1947–54) remembers: 'It was the custom of the college to hold a mission to some parish or group of parishes. The mission was staffed by men in their postgraduate years, and I took part in the autumns of 1952 and 1953. Both missions were held in Holy Trinity, Hull, still recovering from the intense bombing of the city and its dockland ... There was an excellent team of clergy and laity in optimistic mood. Faith our victory indeed! [After ordination, I had a curacy in Hull.] I could not have hoped for a better start to my many years of extraordinary fulfilling and happy ministry.'

'Pastoralia'

So you're preaching tonight at Esh Wining,
And you can't find a text to begin,
You've looked at the lessons, the gospel, epistle,
And you've even tried using a pin.
You thought you might take as your subject
A topic to make them all think –
The Bomb; Common Market; Conversion;
Or if it's expedient to drink.
You've read through the whole of Ezekiel
And Job and the man in the whale,
Could you preach on the need for reunion
Or the order of worship to Baal.
You suddenly wake and you're screaming,
You've just had a terrible fright.
For it's 7 o'clock the next morning
And you preached at Esh Winning last night.

Nehemiah Stone, *Durham Johnian*, January 1962

Social Projects

Johnians have a history of involvement with issues of local concern and have played large parts in social action, protests and raising awareness. J.D.S. Clark remembers: 'The Cuba missile crisis – students praying all over, and CND students sitting down to demonstrate on Palace Green –"Against all tests (nuclear) – AGAINST APATHY".'

Since 1982 Johnians have been heavily involved with Northern Ireland Youth Encounter (NIYE), providing annual holidays for 12- to 14-year-old Protestant and Catholic young

Bishop Linton of Persia, after whom Linton wing is named, was the college's first bishop alumnus.

people to demonstrate how they can cooperate, live together and value each other. St John's provided free accommodation, and activities were based in St Margaret's Church Hall. They held a series of workshops and discussions, in addition to outdoor activities and sightseeing. Fundraising events included a 24-hour sponsored busk in the Market Square (1987) and a sponsored climb of the three highest peaks in Britain within 24 hours.

The Pastoralia scheme began in the 1980s, giving Johnians a chance to get out of the 'Durham bubble' into County Durham. A range of groups of students from both halls provided pastoral support and care to a variety of church-based groups. Activities included visiting elderly people, running youth groups, organizing Sunday Schools, leading and taking part in services, visiting St Margaret's geriatric hospital and so on.

Selected *College Record*s from the 1990s provide excellent representations of global and social action. In 1994 examples include aid to Mostar, a step team in Bolivia, a visit to a Romanian orphanage, seven weeks living in Uganda, a possible link between a theological college in Wuppertal, Germany, and

FAROUK SAYS: "OUT WITH G.B."
WE SAY: "OUT WITH T.B."

John's students on a political rag week float in the mid-1940s.

Support staff raise almost £1,000 for children in need during a sponsored three-legged race down the Bailey in 2004.

Cranmer Hall, a DICCU expedition to a children's home in Poland and the Cranmer crèche in No. 7 South Bailey.

Johnians have also been passionately concerned with environmental issues. In 2000 college was awarded the inaugural 'greenest college' plate.

FAIR TRADE CAMPAIGN

The Just World Shop is a shining example of over 30 years of Johnian's concern for trade justice, with enterprising, visionary students seeing plans come to fruition. The shop was set up in 1976 by a team including Jonathan 'Jonty' Blake and Libby Talbot. Blake remembers: 'One of the enduring legacies of the late 1970s is the Third World Shop, which has become a college institution. I had renounced all worldly goods in support of the poor [and was] often found kipping on the cobwebbed top floor of St John's. Permission was granted for the use of the whole of the top floor of St John's, and a loan was provided. Extraordinary to think they dared to believe people would be willing to climb the endless flights of stairs to reach this retail mission outlet, but people did come in large numbers … At Christmas the bold decision was taken to rent a building and open the shop in the city centre for a month. [Overnight trips to London and Oxford were made for stock.] During the holidays stalls were run at outreach camps, missions and in people's homes. This was trade not aid. I still have a letter from Tearcraft dated April 1978

congratulating the shop on its first successful year and recording that we had purchased well over £2,000 of goods from them, and they were only one of our suppliers. [Profits were donated to charities.] From those somewhat heady and miracle-laden days, the working of the shop has come happily down to earth and it now resides in a more prominent position on the ground floor of the college. I am glad it managed to usurp the old television room.'

Andrew Graystone recalls: 'It was an extraordinary period at St John's. A small group of students didn't just start the shop, they had a genuinely prophetic influence on the university. For instance, they gave up sleeping in beds and slept on the floor as a way of identifying with the Third World. They also rejected college food – which, looking back, was probably quite sensible!'

Originally founded in 1976 in Linton attic, the Just World Shop is now run by a team of volunteers, offering a unique opportunity for Johnians and the wider community to challenge issues of trade justice, and stock up on fair trade snacks and presents.

The Just World Shop's market place stall, 2008.

The shop developed into the 1980s, including weekly 'hunger-lunch' talks – students signed out of college lunches, obtained a rebate and donated it to TEAR Fund to buy refugee meals abroad. A weekly stall was also held in the Students' Union. Bill Marsh recalls: 'From its small beginnings, with £500 worth of stock, the shop has grown considerably, with a current annual turnover of around £3,000 and stock valued at over £4,000' (*Fides*, 1983). David Pain remembers: 'I was the manager of the shop in 1986–7; memories of starting "college reps" to run stalls in other colleges, and both fantastic support within the college and from passers-by on the Bailey. I have worked in development and justice issues ever since, and currently head Christian Aid's Africa division – so I put it down as a formative time for me!'

In 1995 the *College Record* describes the TWS as opening daily, run by 40 students. Some items, newly stocked from Bolivia and India, were bought by students visiting countries in their vacation. Three children were sponsored, and contributions are made to charities. The launch of Café Direct increased sales and provided publicity about fairly traded foods.

The shop was rebranded the Just World Shop in 2000 under the management of Chris Allwood, and it continues to serve an impressive selection of fairly traded goods, providing a city-wide outlet and valuable support to the sponsorship of children in the developing world.

JOHNIANS IN ISRAEL

'The Summer Vacation term of 1929 will long be remembered by me. When early in the year the Principal [Wallis] outlined his plans for this vacation we were entranced at the prospect coming before us: eight weeks in the near East, a week in Cairo, a month in Jerusalem, a few days in Nazareth, a day in Damascus, and a glimpse of Samaria, Constantinople, Athens and Naples! We looked forward to the time of our lives and we were not disappointed.

[During the visit] we were the guests of the Eretz Israel Movement, the Zionist Organisation in Palestine, and we were

Revd Horstead, Bishop of Sierra Leone, just one example of the global reach of St John's College and the tradition of evangelical Anglicanim.

taken by our hosts to some of the Jewish Colonies in Judea and then on to Tel-Aviv. The next day, the Arabs rose up to massacre the Jews. … The Principal told us of the serious situation in the city. He thought we ought to do what we could to help the government. So after tea we went up to the Police headquarters to offer ourselves for duty. We had in our minds the conception of special police which exists in England; the wearing of an armlet and carrying a truncheon and the patrolling on the streets in the true "Robert" style. However, we found that a knowledge of rifles was essential, which meant that ten out of the thirty who volunteered were not accepted. (I was among the ten.)… They were first sent to round up snipers and later to defend Jewish homes. Some of them withstood sieges of several hours' duration, in the course of which a man was wounded. Several of our men had very close shaves and experience marvellous deliverances from danger… [we returned home] wiser men, enriched by many varied experiences.' (J.E. Broadbent, *Durham Johnian*, 1929).

The involvement of St John's students with social concerns strongly reflects the college's Christian, global, missionary focus, which continues well into the 21st century.

Fades Nostril Victoria

Every Cottage needs a motto.
In these PC days of desk tip conductors
With spill chuckers, there is no excuse for spilling
Mistook.

St John's Cottage leads the fjord in Durham.
Fades Nostril Victoria blazes out the massage
Lard and clare,

And members of Crumbly Hole,
As well as the undergarments
In the junior haul, are glade and prude
That the massage has nothing rood innit.

All hale, St John's Cottage!
Tell Victoria that taking drugs will fide her nostra
And she'd better stoop soon!

© David Grieve 2008

The Next 100 Years:
The Principal's Vision

Gazing into the future is not an easy thing. Albert Einstein once wrote to a child anxious about the fate of the world with the words, 'As for the question of the end of it I advise: Wait and see!' Even gazing forward a mere 100 years is just as difficult. As this book shows well, the College would be barely recognizable to those who founded it in 1909. Buildings, students and principals are very different! However, the values and passions stay the same, not least in the vision of a Christian college in a world-class university.

Of course there are lots of visions of the future. However, one vision has particularly excited me in thinking about the future of St John's. This is the biblical image of Zion, the city of God. Now, some will say, surely this cannot be very helpful in thinking about St John's? After all, a popular image of Zion is about creating a state or a place and defending it from outside threats. Indeed, such an image is in the Warchowski brothers' Matrix trilogy, where Zion is the final refuge of human existence and culture and therefore must be defended by force from those who would seek to destroy it. Is this what a Christian college should be, a place of refuge against the inevitable progress of secularism? In many ways a great deal of the literature on both sides of the Atlantic concerning what it means to be a Christian college seem to take this approach. The philosophy of Christian higher education can be defensive, that is resisting modernity, but doing it politely! It can be separatist and arrogant, a view which is quite different to the history and identity of St John's presented in the pages of this book

However, the biblical material on Zion is at times quite different from the view of defence and isolation. There is a strong theme of the gathering of the nations to Zion in a number of Old Testament passages, echoed in the New Testament by the gathering of the nations in the city of God (Rev 21–22). The missiologist Kenneth Cracknell comments 'the nations and peoples will bring into the city their highest achievements of music, art and architecture which have been redeemed, reinvigorated and transformed by God's love'. Zion is a place of joy and delight, freedom and welcome, justice and truth. The Jewish scholar Jon Levenson goes further and notes, 'Zion represents the possibility of meaning above history, out of history, through an opening into the realm of the ideal'.

This view of a place of joyful confidence in the Lord, a place which points forward and embodies that which is to come, and a place of delight and community which draws in all people, seems to me to express all that is good about the history of St John's. However it also challenges us on how we take it forward in our own generation and in the next 100 years. Let me set out my dream of what St John's College might look like as we build on the last 100 years.

First, we need to be a place of formation of the whole person. A number of commentators in higher education have recently pointed out the danger of fragmentation in knowledge, between teaching and research, and between the formation of character and the need to pass exams. Others argue that education for delight has been replaced by education for capability. Of course we need to be realists and higher education must be good value for money both for students and society as a whole. However, Durham's collegiate system is ideally placed to address this fragmentation, and St John's as a Christian college offers not just the importance of spirituality but also a context for spirituality in forming the whole person. We need to demonstrate that joyful confidence in engaging the Christian faith with academic studies, to speak of vocation rather than just employability, and to encourage a delight in learning as a gift from God. At the same time we need to humbly offer our distinct Christian understanding while maintaining openness to staff and students of all backgrounds and beliefs, an openness which welcomes all and learns from all. It is easy for students and staff to feel marginalized and neglected in the emerging market-led, budget-constrained, assurance-concerned context of higher education. This is on top of the challenges of transition which marks the annual rhythm of the college community. We need to be a place of support and development of students and staff.

Second, we do need to be a place of excellence for all. A Christian college has no excuse to be mundane or to be lazy in striving for excellence. St John's College has the immense privilege of being an integral part of one of the world's top research-led universities. The pages of this history are a reminder both of achievements in academic excellence but also the challenges of academic excellence. This is not about building a culture of elitism, but to provide the atmosphere where students and staff, both academic and support, can grow with confidence and passion towards their full potential. Thus, St John's must be a supportive structure for academic staff and students to excel in research and learning, alongside striving for excellence in sport, drama, art and music.

In particular, I hope and pray that St John's will continue to be a centre of excellence within the theological training landscape. The achievements of Cranmer Hall and the Wesley Study Centre have been remarkable in forming outstanding leaders for the church, people who are making a difference to the local communities in which they are set as well as at national and international levels.

Third, St John's is called to be prophetic, a place which points forward and embodies that which is to come. We have been privileged to be part of a college which has been at the forefront of the fairtrade movement, the theological training of women and Christian communication. We need to see our role as prophetic servant to the university, to the church and to our culture. To be a place of leadership in thinking, training and transformation of society is what our history calls us to.

Finally, we need to be a college. We are not simply a hall of residence or indeed a vicar factory! A college is a place of scholarship, rich community, innovation, critical resistance, security and challenge, hospitality, diversity and unity. St John's is a place of dynamic complexity, finding its true identity in being a college. As a college of Durham University we can give much but we also can receive much. As a Christian college we should not be defensive or self seeking, but embrace the next 100 years with joyful confidence in the Lord Jesus.

Principal David Wilkinson, Ruth Etchells and David Day in the college's Etchells' Room at David Wilkinson's welcome service, 17th October 2006.

"The vocation of St John's College is to be a community of learning in which people flourish together abundantly for life, service and leadership in church and society."

David A. Wilkinson

List of Subscribers

Richard Allum
Ian Andrew
Emma Arnold
Keith Atkinson
Penny Bainbridge (née Lockhart)
Miss Janet Margaret Baker
Peter Banister
Jodie-Hannah Barnes
Revd Dr and Mrs Bartlett
Tim Bartlett
Sallie Bassham
Katie Bell (née Adlard)
Wendy Bell
Revd David Benge
Revd Gilliam Belford
Peter Birdsall
Richard Blackburn
Miss Clare Bliss
Stefanie Boehm
Revd Peter Bowes
Alison Bradshaw and the Catering Team
Father Bill Braviner
Revd Robert Breckles
Helen Brett
Elizabeth Broad (née Bradley)
Harry Broadbent
A.W. Brooke
Janine Broome
The Rt Revd Mark Bryant
Nathaniel and Katie Buckingham
Charlotte Buckley
John and Maria Burniston
Alexandra Cameron
Revd Stan Carter
Revd David Catterall
Dr Julian and Mrs Barbara Chadwick
Charles M.D. Chalkly-Maber
Robert Chalmers
Hilary Chapman (née Robson)
Janet Chapman (née Craven)
Philip Chetwood and Revd Noah
    Chetwood
Robert Cheyne

Richard and Anne Child
Alan R. Clark
David Clark
Eric George Clarkson
Daniel Clayton
William David Clemmey
John Cockerton
Revd Paul C.N. Conder
Revd Prof. and Mrs Chris Cook
Michael J. Cooke
Alice Cooper (née Keech)
Lucy Cornell
Dr John M. Court
Frank Cranmer
Revd Geoffrey Crees
Mrs Linda Cross
Alan Crossley
Revd Elizabeth Cummings
The Rt Revd Ian Cundy
Ruth Curry
Canon Adrian Daffern
Andrew Dalgleish
Alan Davis
Roger de Ste Croix
Alan Denison
Peter C. Denton
William Robert Domeris
Judith Dunthorne
Robert Eabry
Sylvia and Patrick Earle
Roger Eastman
Rt Revd Chris Edmondson,
    Bishop of Bolton
The Very Revd Dr John Edmondson
Revd Joseph P. Edwardson
Miss Kathryn M. Elmer
Henry C.S. Elston
Dr Ruth Etchells
Revd John F. Fairclough
Revd Gerald Farleigh
Gavin Alexander Forrest
Rt Revd Dr Peter Forster
Revd and Mrs K.M. Fraser-Smith

Ben Fuller
Bob Fyall
Andrew Gandon
Rt Revd Michael F. Gear
Jane Ghosh
Derek Gibson
Matt Giles
Kate Godfree
Sophie Godfree
Vanessa Gould
Tim Gray
Revd David Grieve
Revd Jane Grieve (née Pierssené)
Matthew Gunby
Dr Keith J. Hacking
Revd Richard Haigh
David and Stephanie Halse
Canon John M. Hancock
Dr Peter Harland
Eric John Harris
Mrs Peter Harrison
Ben Harrison
Elena Haste
Tracey Hatcher (née Payne)
Michael Havell
Naomi Hawkins
Matthew Healy
Jenny M. Heath
Emma Catherine Herd
    (née Buckingham)
Revd Dobson Heron
David Hill
Canon Richard Hill
Mr John and Revd Judy Hirst
Sue Hobson and the Housekeeping Team
David Hocking
Martin John Hodgetts
Stanley Holbrooke-Jones
Richard Holdridge
Jim Holland
Prof. Sir Frederick Holliday
Nigel Hollington
Lionel G. Holmes

Tim Honeywill
Revd Tim Horsington
David M. Houghton
Revd David H. Howarth
Olivia Howland
The Very Revd John C. Hughes
Michelle Hussey (née Lavender)
Jeremy and Daphne Hutchinson
Rebecca Hutton (née Tomlinson)
Sean James Illing
Michalakis Ioannides
Mr G. Jagger
Revd Jeremy James
Bob Jameson
Henry P. Jansma
Matthew Jenkins
Emilia V.A. McAllister Jepps
Harriet Ruth Johnston
Mrs C. Jones
David V. Jones
Revd Oliver Kendall
Lucy Knight
Emanuel O. Kolade
James Lamb
Revd Ronald Lancaster MBE MA FRSC
Georgie Lane-Godfrey
Matthew Lavis
Christine Leahy
Dr John S. Lee
Aled W. Lewis
The Venerable Ralph Lindley BA CBE
Canon Robert Lindsay
Joseph Edward Little
Rachael Loades
Revd Ken Loraine
Michael and Emma Macey
Duncan Mackenzie
L.H.W. March
C.P. Marshall
Helen Marshall
Revd A.B. Martin-Doyle
Emma Matthews
The Venerable Bob Metcalf
Douglas Michell
Revd Alan Middleton
D. David Miller MA
Revd A.J. Millyard
Revd Stuart Mitchell
Revd Peter Moger
The Revd Canon Dr Nicholas Molony
Revd David Monteith
Revd Peter Newing

David and Jane Newsome
Victor George Nickless
Amelia Nickols
Revd Linda Norman
Danielle O'Hagan
John Oliver
Revd David Olsson
David Osborne
Sarah Elizabeth Page
Revd Michael Pain
Francis J. Parkinson
Peter M. Philips
Mrs S.D. Pounde
Prebendary Lawrence Price
Sarah Price
Revd Tony Price
Rhys Pullen
A. Quinn
Martin Randall
Revd Arthur Rhodes
Neil Rider
Mary E. Francis
Mrs B. Riley
The Venerable Peter Rivett
Richard A. Roberts
Revd Michael and Revd Andrea Roberts
Canon Paul S. Robertson
Neil Robinson
Canon John Rogan
Julia Margareta Maria Ruckert
Canon Jim Rushton
Revd Canon A.E.H. Rutter
Ben Salter
Rt Revd Frank Sargeant
Jeremy Sargent
Dr Kuhan Satkunanayagam
Rt Revd John Saxbee
Rachel Scarfe
Felix M. Schubert
Robert and Sally Scott-Biggs
Nigel Sherlock
Timothy G. Shock
Simon T. Shreeve
Michael Shrewsbury
Adrian Smith
Revd Barbara Smith
Maddie Smith
Mark W. Smith
Conor Snowden
William Snowley
Charlotte South (née Owen) and
    Rebecca Scott (née South)

The Venerable Leslie Stanbridge
Simon Stevens
Helen and Willie Stewart
Chrissy Stoodley
A.E. Storm
Loren and Lois Stuckenbruck
Revd John Swallow
Cathy Swan
Sheila Swarbrick (née Pite)
Manfred Sydow
David Tait
John R. Tate
Ian Taylor
E.L. Temple
Revd Brian Tetley
Matthew Thurland
Julia G.L. Tolley
David Tomlinson
Canon Desmond Treanor
The Very Revd Marc Trickey
The Rt Revd Michael Turnbull CBE
Leslie Turner
Mr Adam Tyrrell
Kevin Christopher Roy Tyson
Jonathan Ullmer
David William Vail
Tony Vigars
Mr Adrian Vincent
Robert J.D. Wainwright
G.T. Wakefield
John L. Wall
Simon A. Walsh
The Venerable Geoffrey Walton
David Warrington
G. Peter Wedgwood
Christopher Weller
Robert C. Wells
John David Wheeldon
Cassian Wheeler
Diana Whelan
John and Tom Wickson
Georgina Wilczek (née Luck)
David and Alison Wilkinson
John Wilkinson
Geoffrey Willett
Rosie and David Wills
Revd Sue Wing
David Winston
Canon Brian Wisken
Mrs Mary A.J. Worley
Katharine Louise Unsworth Wray
Timothy and Molly Yates

Index

Acknowledgements

Richard Adams: 86 (bottom r); Alan & Helen Bartlett: 51 (top), 117 (top r); Amabel Craig: 8-9, 88 (bottom), 97 (top centre), 112 (right); David Day: 79, 90 (top l), 97 (bottom l); Alan Denison: 19 (l), 20 (l), 85 (insert), 110 (bottom r); Durham University Archive, Palace Green Special Collections: St John's College Archive: Endpapers & 12 (arranged by Amabel Craig, photographed by Kate Weightman), 14 (top & bottom), 15 (top), 17 (r), 18 (r from *The Record* newspaper 1913), 31 (top l), 34 (l), 35, 36, 46, 47, 48, 51 (r), 58-9, 60 (bottom), 61 (centre), 65 (r), 66 (top r), 67 (bottom r & insert), 68 (middle), 72 (r), 73 (r), 75, 80 (r), 86 (top), 87 (top l), 91 (bottom r), 92 (top l), 94 (top r), 95 (top r) 102 (insert), 103 (top l), 104 (top l), 108 (bottom l), 111 (top l), 117 (top l); Ruth Etchells: 41, 43, 44 (top & bottom), 45 (insert), 70 (r), 90 (centre); Luke Garnham: 70 (centre), 90 (bottom r), 92 (bottom left), 94 (bottom), 104 (bottom r), 105 (bottom l); Matt Giles: 93 (r); David & Jane Grieve: 34 (r), 39 (top & bottom), 97 (far left); Hazel Harrison: 26 (centre), 27 (r), 30 (r), 32(l), 35 (insert); Martin Hodgetts: 119 (bottom r), 120 (top); Stanley Holbrooke-Jones: 28 (r); David Houghton: 105 (l); St John's College: 8-9, 13 (centre), 16(l), 17 (l), 20-21 (centre), 22 (l), 28 (l), 49 (l), 51 (top l), 73 (l), 106-7, 117 (bottom r), 121 (insert); R. Hunter / Skyscan.co.uk (bottom): 8-9; Margaret Masson: 50 (l), 74, 97 (far l); Kippa Matthews: 2, 15 (bottom l & r), 56-57, 62 (r), 63 (l), 65(l), 67 (top l), 71 (r), 80, 89 (top), 105 (top), 109 (top), 112 (l), 115 (r), 121 insert; Arthur Millyard: 70 (top r), 118 (bottom l); Al Muir: 100 (bottom r); Rosemary Nixon: 31 (r), 38, 45 (bottom), 62 (l), 87 (l & r), 72 (r), 73 (r), 75, 80 (r), 86 (top), 87 (top l), 104 (top r); John Oliver: 60 (top); Roddy Peters: 51 (bottom), 118 (top r); Tom Pember-Finn: 108 (bottom); Jonathan Pye: 95 (bottom r); Neil Robinson: 26 (l); Felix Schubert: back cover; Leslie Stanbridge: 60 (top), 84, 108 (top l); Chloe Starr: 53 (r), 61 (left & far r), 88 (top l); Lois Stuckenbruck: 96 (bottom l), 100 (top), 114 (bottom); Phil Thomas: 89 (bottom r), 93 (top r); Desmond Treanor: 96 (top r); Triptych Design: 65 (bottom l), 76 (r), 77 (r), 102 (centre), 110 (centre); Michael Turnbull: 6, 35 (insert); Georgina Wilczeck: 65 (r), 98-9; Joy Wishlade: 29 (r); Matthew Wilson: 7, 21(r), 23 (l & r), 40 (bottom), 50 (lower r), 63 (bottom), 64, 66 (r), 68 (top & bottom l), 69 (top l), 70 (l), 71(insert), 76 (l), 78